Soups and Starters

Marika Hanbury Tenison

Soups and Starters

GRANADA
London Toronto Sydney New York

Granada Publishing Limited
Frogmore, St Albans, Herts AL2 2NF
and
3 Upper James Street, London W1R 4BP
Suite 405, 4th Floor, 866 United Nations Plaza, New York,
NY 10017, USA
117 York Street, Sydney, NSW 2000, Australia
100 Skyway Avenue, Rexdale, Ontario M9W 3A6, Canada
PO Box 84165, Greenside, 2034 Johannesburg, South Africa
61 Beach Road, Auckland, New Zealand

First published as *Soups and Hors d'Oeuvres* by Penguin Books Ltd 1969
Reprinted 1969
This edition published by Granada Publishing 1980

ISBN 0 246 11302 2

Printed in Great Britain by
Fakenham Press Ltd, Fakenham, Norfolk

GRANADA ®
GRANADA PUBLISHING ®

This book is dedicated to *Maidenwell*
and everyone there who helps to make the system work

Contents

Foreword to the
New Edition

First courses to me are the spice of life. We all have a favourite course; many people may prefer the main course with its hearty meat, fish, poultry and game dishes, others may long for the sweetness of the pudding course, but for me it is the first course which offers some of the greatest pleasures of both table and kitchen. Starters tend to be relatively quick and simple to make; the artist in me takes pleasure in their arrangement; preparing and cooking them is always rewarding and serving them sets the tone for the whole of a meal. If the first course is a success the rest of the meal will almost always follow in its footsteps.

Starters include soups, fish dishes, egg dishes, concoctions of cheese, salads, simple titbits and more lavish pastry appetizers, each one with literally hundreds of variations. There are cold soups, hot soups and spiced soups; sea food cocktails and, best of all, a dazzling choice of cold dishes that go to make up a traditional hors d'oeuvre. There is room for experimentation, for unusual combinations and for inspiration on the part of the cook. What is more, the majority of the dishes can be made in advance, needing only to be chilled or heated through before being served. Many of the dishes can also be served, in their own right, as a main course for a light meal and most are surprisingly economical as they do not have to rely on expensive cuts of meat, poultry, game or fish for their main ingredients.

A first course deserves every minute of the time you spend on it: the home-made stock that makes all the difference to a soup; the carefully thought out garnishing that contrasts or complements the other ingredients; and the meticulous attention that is paid to chopping, slicing and shredding ingredients. With a home-made stock you always give a soup a flavour that is entirely your own; a little chopped chervil, lovage or parsley will perform miracles for the look of a tomato, beetroot or pale coloured soup and nothing can be nicer on a hot day than a salad that is composed of carefully and evenly julienned ingredients in a home-made mayonnaise.

One could not hope to cover, in a book of this size, all the first courses known to the culinary world as there must be approaching a million of them that are indigenous to the great cuisines of the world. In this book I have concentrated on those I particularly enjoy myself and, perhaps above all, through necessity, on those that are on the less expensive side. Not for most of us the extravagancies of caviar, oysters and smoked salmon, simple as they are to serve but, on the other hand, the first course can play a major role in cutting down the cost of a dinner party as a whole. A simple but sustaining first course like a good nourishing soup, which still costs remarkably little, a salad of broad beans or even well-flavoured stuffed eggs helps to take the edge off your guests' appetites, puts them in a good mood and means that you can often economize on the vastly more expensive main course.

During the time I wrote this book my family were subjected to six months of trying out first courses which they had not only as starters but frequently as the main course too, and my dinner parties consisted of a dozen or more first courses which I tried out on my guests and asked for their comments; no one complained and everyone, like me, liked the recipes which appear on the following pages.

Some golden rules apply to the serving of soups and hors d'oeuvres and they are virtually a guarantee of success: soups must be served either hot or cold and that means in hot or cold soup plates or bowls, as nothing is more off-putting than a tepid liquid to start a meal; so heat your bowls or put them in a refrigerator before pouring in the soup.

Garnishing is always an important part of a good soup or an hors d'oeuvre. It takes so little time to fry up some golden, crisp *croûtons* for a bowl of soup, to chop some chives, parsley, chervil or lovage to sprinkle over a cold hors d'oeuvre, and a few thin strips of pimento and some thinly slivered black olives can add both colour and attraction to a hot dish. Simple little touches like these, which show you have taken trouble and cared for the presentation of your food, make those who eat it doubly appreciative of something which, while it may not be expensive, is nevertheless truly delicious.

June 1979   Marika Hanbury Tenison
                                                         Maidenwell
                                                            Cornwall

Unless otherwise indicated all recipes are for four servings. Both imperial and metric weights and measures are given in this book. Either should give perfect results but they are not equivalents and therefore not interchangeable. Do not mix imperial and metric weights and measures in the same recipe. Use either one or the other.

CHAPTER ONE

PREPARING & COOKING FIRST COURSES

Obviously a whole new range of cooking utensils is not necessary for the making of first courses but certain items, although not essential, do help and save time.

So much of the preparation of first courses consists of chopping that a really good selection of sharp knives is invaluable. Knives are no good without a sharpener. Having tried every type I still find the best is the old fashioned upright sharpener with a steel inset through which the knife is run back and forth. Many recipes call for puréeing; this can usually be done through a fine sieve but much less trouble is to use a Mouli food mill: the French firm Mouli produce a wide range of these gadgets which are not expensive. The largest food mill has a selection of plates which can be used for anything from sieving to shredding. Pâtés are best made in a proper earthenware terrine dish with a fitted lid. These come in all sizes and make useful small casserole dishes.

KITCHEN EQUIPMENT
CUTTING, SLICING AND CHOPPING

Three knives are essential and it is worth lashing out on them. Good quality knives last for ever and keep their sharpness far longer than cheap ones. Choose a long and well pointed carving knife about 23 cm (9 inches) long, a medium knife of about 15–18 cm (6–7 inches) and a small one viciously sharp and pointed.

A potato peeler helps in shaving off orange and lemon rind, and of course carrot and potato peel.

For chopping anything from onions to anchovies, the French have invented the hachoir or mezzaluna, a curved bladed two handled knife which chops with a see saw motion. This is a wonderful tool and far more efficient than most of the patent chopping gadgets on the market.

Kitchen scissors make short work of removing the rinds from bacon and trimming the edges off anything from pastry to poached eggs.

Egg slicers are cheap and neat. I have both kinds, one cuts the egg into thin even slices, the other cuts them into eight.

A parsley mincer reduces parsley and mint to very small pieces. The job can be done just as well with a pair of scissors and a mug.

A Universal slicer – a wooden frame with a number of adjustable blades with patterned edges – slices cucumber into wafer thin slithers and produces neat matchstick lengths of vegetables.

For all chopping and cutting you need a board. Wooden ones are vastly superior to all the rather chichi plastic ones.

MIXING, BEATING AND WHISKING

One cannot have too many wooden spoons of all shapes and sizes from very small ones for sauces, to very large ones for soups.

A hand electric mixer is useful for all mixing and beating. A rotary whisk does the job especially well but not so fast.

A small wire whisk is invaluable for making all sauces, especially those liable to curdle.

PURÉEING, STRAINING, AND BLENDING

One of the greatest kitchen assets to have appeared during the last decade is the food processor which has replaced, in my opinion, both the mixer and liquidizer. A good food processor not only slices, shreds, juliennes and grates but also purées (drain ingredients of excess liquid before processing). A good investment for anyone who enjoys cooking.

It is also necessary to have two sieves, a large, coarse one and a hair sieve and for general bashing and pounding of spices there is still nothing to beat an old-fashioned pestle and mortar.

Some of the most useful kitchen equipment need not be expensive. An article I use frequently is a large cheap wire straining spoon available from professional kitchen shops, which is invaluable for lifting fried food from deep fat and for draining poached eggs.

COOKING ON THE STOVE

Who can cook anything without saucepans? Quality counts here and good ones are always worth paying for. Cheap pans cook unevenly and burn easily. Have a large thick bottomed pan for stocks, a medium one and a small, preferably non-stick pan, for sauces. Non-stick pans take the agony out of washing up but take care never to use a sharp wire spoon or whisk as the non-stick coating scratches easily and is expensive to re-coat.

Large or whole fish need a fish kettle. They come in all sizes and apart from their obvious function I find them useful for flower arrangements.

Steaming can be done in a colander over a saucepan but a proper steamer makes things easier and has the advantage of having a well fitted lid. In the same way it is possible to improvise and use a basin over a saucepan of water as a double boiler, but a proper double boiler is best. I long for someone to invent a glass top to a double boiler so that one can see what the water below is up to.

Keep a special frying pan for making omelettes and pancakes. This should not be washed or scrubbed but carefully wiped out with a soft dry cloth.

Frying pans must be absolutely flat on the bottom to ensure even cooking all over the pan. Buy one that is really large enough. Fried food quickly loses its flavour and, whenever possible, all frying should be done at the same time and not in batches.

Deep frying is made easier by using a proper fryer with a fitted basket.

Forget egg poachers; they don't poach, they steam the eggs.

COOKING IN THE OVEN

Pyrex makes a good range of baking dishes at a reasonable price. More expensive but very attractive to look at and to serve from are a range of French fireproof dishes.

Soufflés can be made in any straight sided dish but better results are obtained by using a proper soufflé dish. Buy one of a $\frac{3}{4}$–1 litre ($1\frac{1}{2}$–2 pint) capacity.

Earthenware ramekins or cocottes can be used as butter dishes, ashtrays or for baking individual soufflés and are indispensable for so many of those cheap and delicious oeuf en cocotte or baked egg dishes.

Flan dishes and patty cases are now made with a covering of non-stick substance making cleaning much easier and doing away with the boring chore of greasing cases before lining them with pastry.

Have at least two earthenware terrines in different sizes for making and serving pâtés and potted meats.

COLD DISHES

Lettuce leaves and all salad greenery need a good wash. A collapsible wire basket makes draining and drying the leaves a lot quicker and easier.

So many cold dishes are set in moulds or shapes that it is useful to have a wide range of these. The cheapest are just as good as the more expensive ones.

Keep used Stilton jars, earthenware marmalade and mincemeat pots for refilling with pastes, pâtés and potted meats.

ESSENTIAL DISPOSABLES

Two of the greatest contributions to kitchen efficiency have been the inventions of aluminium foil and absorbent kitchen paper. Keep plenty of both within easy reach. Use foil instead of lids, for sealing and baking, and to keep things in the fridge or larder. Lettuce washed and well drained and lightly wrapped in aluminium foil will keep for days in a refrigerator.

Kitchen paper does a million jobs from draining the fat from fried food (crumple up the paper first) to mopping up spilt liquids.

ADDITIONAL INDISPENSABLES

Pastry making is an arduous job but a marble slab does make it easier. So does a pastry cutter, a series of curved wire blades which quickly reduces the flour and fat to the consistency of coarse breadcrumbs.

Metal tongs are useful for turning food that is being fried and for lifting bouquets garnis,etc., from stocks or soups.

A small, very sharp, curved knife helps to cut radish roses and other shapes for garnishing.

A garlic press is essential for anyone who uses garlic.

A good knife sharpener, a collection of screw top jars and a pastry brush complete my list of essentials.

STORING FOOD

It is surprising how long perishable food will keep if properly treated, but horrifying how quickly it goes off if not. Aluminium foil and cling wrapping are great assets in preserving. So are those polythene containers with tight fitting lids. Many foods like to breathe, they can be lightly covered with a foil or cling wrapping, but should never be sealed or tightly wrapped in paper. Some foods let off strong odours which quickly taint other perishable goods. Melon, cheese, onions and anything with garlic are among the worst offenders. They should all be well wrapped before being put in the refrigerator.

The refrigerator is the best place to store most things if you plan to keep them for a few days, but it is worth remembering that the top of the refrigerator is the coldest part, and eggs, cheeses and all salad stuffs should be kept at the very bottom.

If you are short of cool storage space, an electric fan (inexpensive to run) can be a most invaluable help in hot weather. It will keep the air circulating, creating a draught and so lowering the temperature.

METHODS OF STORING INDIVIDUAL GOODS TO PRESERVE THEM FOR THE LONGEST POSSIBLE TIME

DAIRY GOODS

Butter. Store in the refrigerator – keep well wrapped. Salted butter keeps better than unsalted butter.

Cheese. Store in a cool place – wrap in foil, cling wrapping or greaseproof paper.

Milk. Store in a refrigerator, reseal the top with foil once it has been opened.

Cream and sour cream. Store in a refrigerator, reseal once opened.

Eggs. Store in the least cold area of the refrigerator. Eggs should be at room temperature before being used for cooking. Store hard boiled eggs in water in a cool place or refrigerator.

MEAT, FISH AND POULTRY. Remove wrapping from all raw meats and fish unless the product is sealed in a special polythene sachet. Re-wrap lightly with foil or cling wrapping. Store in the coldest part of the refrigerator. Wrap cold meat, fish and poultry in foil or cling wrapping. Store in the refrigerator. Store pâtés and terrines in the refrigerator well sealed with aluminium foil.

SALAD STUFFS. Wash salads and dry well before storing in a self sealing polythene container or wrapping in foil. Store in the least cold area of the refrigerator. Watercress and celery should be kept with their stalks in water which must be changed daily.

FRUIT. Store in a cool larder or in the least cold area of the refrigerator. Wrap melon, pineapple and any heavily odoured fruit well. Bananas should not be kept in a refrigerator.

Ripen fruit on a sunny windowsill or in an airing cupboard.

Sprinkle cut avocado pears with lemon juice to preserve their colour.

FRUIT JUICE. Keep fruit juices in a covered jug in the refrigerator. Use tinned fruit juice within 48 hours.

TINNED GOODS. Store tinned goods in a cool place. Remove all foodstuff from a tin that has been opened. Store it in a refrigerator and use within 48 hours.

BOTTLED GOODS. Keep all bottled goods in a cool place. Opened bottles of olives, capers, gherkins, etc. should be stored in a refrigerator. Always reseal bottles tightly after use.

Salad dressing can be made in quite large quantities and kept in a tightly sealed bottle in a cool place.

DRIED GOODS. Keep pastas, cereals and dried herbs in a really dry cupboard.

SAUCES, PÂTÉS, PASTES, ETC., IN TUBES. Tubes can be kept in a cool larder but once they have been opened, they must be stored in a refrigerator.

GARLIC AND FRESH HERBS. Keep garlic in a really dry place out of contact with other food stuff.

Stand fresh herbs with their stems in water.

THE STORE CUPBOARD

Many basic and additional ingredients of a wide selection of first courses can be kept in the store cupboard, making a large variety of first courses and hors d'oeuvres readily available at short notice. Replace the goods as you use them.

Keep a basic supply of:

Tinned Goods
    Soups to use as bases
    Consommé and vichyssoise

Madrilène soup (chicken and tomato consommé)
Anchovy fillets
Crab
Herring fillets
Minced clams
Mussels
Salmon
Sardines
Shrimps
Tuna fish
Baby beetroot
Italian tomatoes
Mushrooms
Pâté
Pimento (sweet red pepper)
Spinach
Sweetcorn
Tomato purée

Bottled Goods or those in Jars
Capers
Cider vinegar
Dijon mustard
Horseradish sauce
Mayonnaise (choose one that is made with lemon juice)
Mushroom ketchup
Olive oil (I buy mine from Boots where it is of especially
    good quality, but the least expensive way to buy oil is in
    a two-gallon tin)
Olives
Pickled beetroot
Pickled cucumbers
Pickled gherkins
Pickled onions
A selection of pickles and chutneys
Smoked cod's roe
Sunflower oil
Tabasco sauce

Tarragon vinegar
Tomato ketchup
White or red wine vinegar
White wine for cooking
Worcester sauce

Dried Herbs, Spices, etc.
Bay leaves
Breadcrumbs
Dried herbs and spices of every variety
Ready made bouquet garni
Peppercorns, ground white and black pepper
Cayenne and paprika pepper
Salt (table and crystals)

Goods in Tubes
Horseradish
French mustard
Tomato purée

Goods in Packets
Dried mushrooms
Dried peas and beans
Grated Parmesan cheese
Lentils
Pasta – Italian only
Rice – Patna only

In the Refrigerator

	Storage Time
Double cream	4 days
Single cream	4 days
Sour cream	10 days
Cream cheese or Boursin	10 days
Cheddar cheese	2 weeks
Gruyère cheese	2 weeks
Yoghurt	7 days

THE USE OF HERBS, SPICES, AND FLAVOURING IN THE COOKING OF FIRST COURSES

Whenever possible use fresh herbs in your cooking. If you cannot get fresh herbs soften the dried variety in a little warm water before using them. Dried herbs quickly lose their flavour once the container has been opened so only buy small quantities at a time.

Nothing ruins a dish as easily as too much flavouring – always under- rather than over-season and remember that since you are continually tasting a dish as you cook it, the taste will be less strong to you than to those who will eat it for the first time.

I prefer to use pure olive oil, but this is now so expensive that I have resorted to using sunflower oil, which I find to be the best alternative. And I always use freshly ground black pepper instead of the ground white variety which seems to me to have little or no taste. Pepper, like coffee beans, should be ground as it is required.

ANCHOVY ESSENCE. A strong essence made from puréed anchovies. Use in fish dishes and sauces.

BASIL. Use in soups, and in all tomato dishes.

BAY LEAVES. One of the most widely used herbs. It is an essential ingredient in the bouquet garni and is indispensable in the cooking of most pâtés and terrines.

BOUQUET GARNI. The mixed herb flavouring used in the cooking of most soups and many sauces. A bay leaf, 2 sprigs of parsley and a sprig of thyme are tied together and removed before the dish is served. The herbs can be tied in a small muslin bag and it is now possible to buy these muslin bags ready made up.

CAPERS. These are pickled in vinegar and used in sauces and as a garnish.

CARDAMOM SEED. Use when pickling and marinading. Ground cardamom is delicious sprinkled over iced melon.

CAYENNE PEPPER. A hot red pepper. Use sparingly in hot sauces and serve with raw oysters.

CELERY SALT. A useful flavouring for soups and fruit juice cocktails.

CHILLI PEPPER. A very hot pepper made from dried red chillis. Widely used in Mexican cooking and a useful addition to many egg dishes. Use very sparingly.

CHUTNEY. Traditional accompaniment to curry and cold meats. There are hundreds of varieties. Finely chopped chutney is useful as a flavouring for some sauces and mousses.

CUMIN. Another hot spice used in curries.

CURRY POWDER. A prepared combination of hot herbs and spices which can be bought in varying degrees of hotness. Only buy small tins of curry powder as it loses its flavour quickly once the tin has been opened.

CURRY PASTE. Stronger than curry powder and should be used sparingly. I find it much easier to blend than the powdered variety.

DILL. This is one of my favourite herbs. The feathery leaves and the seeds are used in pickling and are delicious in fish dishes and with vegetables. It is far more widely used in Scandinavian and Baltic countries than in the rest of Europe.

DRIED MUSHROOMS. These are usually the toadstool varieties (Cèpes or Boletus). They have a very strong almost meaty flavour and should be used (sparingly) in soups and sauces.

GARLIC. One of the most important flavourings of all. Use cloves of garlic and never garlic salt, essence or powder. The quantity you use depends a lot on taste but bear in mind that some people really do detest the taste so go easy if you are unsure. Use in the flavouring of sauces, soups, in the cooking of most tomato dishes and in salads.

The easiest way to crush a clove of garlic is to use a garlic press. Do not peel the garlic before putting it through the press.

HARVEY SAUCE. A strong salty sauce. Use to flavour soups and sauces.

HORSERADISH. Grate fresh horseradish and mix with vinegar and cream. Soak dried horseradish in a little warm water before using. Use as a flavouring in sauces and mayonnaise.

JUNIPER BERRIES. Use crushed berries in pâtés and terrines.

MACE. Ground mace is an aromatic spice made from the outer casing of the nutmeg. Use sparingly in pâtés, terrines and with potted meats and fish.

MARJORAM. A herb of the mint family. Use in sauces and soups.

MINT. Dried mint is almost flavourless. Use fresh chopped mint with melon and cucumber dishes.

MUSTARD (ENGLISH). Use for sauces and in salad dressings.

MUSTARD (FRENCH). The bright yellow Dijon brand with a faint tinge of tarragon has by far the best flavour. The English imitations are a muddy colour and not worth using. Use in sauces and salad dressings.

NUTMEG. Use ground nutmeg in some soups and with vegetables.

OLIVE AND SUNFLOWER OIL. Use pure olive oil for dressings and sauces but the less expensive sunflower oil for shallow and deep frying.

PARSLEY. Dried parsley has very little taste. Use fresh parsley as a flavouring for sauces, in soups and as a garnish.

PEPPER (BLACK). Use freshly ground black pepper whenever possible. The flavour is much more pronounced than that of the ready-ground variety.

PEPPER (WHITE). Less strong than black pepper. Use in white sauces where black pepper would spoil the appearance of the dish.

ROSEMARY. A strongly flavoured herb. Use sparingly in soups and sauces.

SAFFRON. A yellow spice. Use sparingly in soups and to colour rice.

SAGE. Use in small quantities to flavour soups and tomato dishes.

SALT. The partially refined sea salt is far better than the ordinary table salt. It can be ground in a salt mill or powdered in a pestle and mortar.

SOUR CREAM. A cultured cream that gives a delicious flavour to many soups and sauces. If you cannot get sour cream mix lemon juice with fresh cream.

TABASCO SAUCE. A very very hot sauce. Use in drops. Add to some mousses, sea food dressings and to tomato juice.

TARRAGON. One of the best herbs. Use in salads and sauces.

THYME. One of the ingredients of a bouquet garni.

THYME, LEMON. Use with egg dishes and grilled shellfish.

TOMATO PURÉE. Strong concentrated tomato flavouring from Italy. Use to increase the flavour of tomato in tomato dishes.

VINEGAR. Malt vinegar is very harsh and should only be used in pickling. Use white and red wine vinegar and tarragon wine vinegar for all marinades and sauces.

WORCESTER SAUCE. A strong bottled sauce. Use in drops as a flavouring for sea food cocktails, tomato juice and in devilled dishes.

WINE AND OTHER DRINKS WITH FIRST COURSES

Gone, thank heavens, are the rigid days of 'sherry with the soup, white wine with the fish and red wine with the meat'. Within reason any wine can be drunk with any food nowadays without eyebrows being raised and hands held up in horror. In general dry white wines do go best with most of the first courses and a dry sherry is delicious with soups. However if you prefer drinking red wine throughout the meal I am the last person to suggest that you should not.

It is worth remembering that spirits, especially whisky, can have disastrous effects on some people if they are drunk while eating shellfish.

FIRST COURSES FOR BUFFET PARTIES

Buffet parties will never fail to be an entertainment popular with the hostess. Eating standing up may be uncomfortable for the guest, but for the hostess it solves all the problems of getting a large number of people 'over' at one time, the worry of how to seat them and the problem of how to serve them.

The first course plays an enormous part in any buffet party and some combinations of the dishes in this book, served with a selection of salads, would make adequate and attractive main courses for any party.

Remember that people eat less standing up than they do sitting and at a party where the food is laid out and the guests help themselves, appearance and arrangement are of great importance. Any food that is eaten standing up should be cut small enough to be eaten with a fork.

Hostesses will want to serve dishes that can be prepared well in advance.

A FEW SUGGESTIONS OF FIRST OR MAIN COURSE DISHES FOR PARTIES

Poached salmon or sea trout
Rich salmon mould
Rose sole
Fish mousse
Mixed fish salad
Good Friday salad
Crab mousse
Prawn salad
Scampi salad
Pâtés and terrines
Potted pigeon
Quiches served hot or cold
Cold curried eggs

A FEW MISCELLANEOUS HINTS

Lemons and oranges produce more juice if they are slightly warmed in an oven before squeezing.

Butter can be clarified by being heated in a pan until it foams and then poured through muslin.

Spaghetti and rice will not boil over if a knob of butter is added to the water.

Melons and avocado pears can be tested for ripeness by lightly pressing the stalk end of the fruit. The end should be slightly soft.

Frozen food can be kept frozen for up to one hour if it is very well wrapped in newspaper.

Steel, unless stainless, should not be used to cut fruit or salad stuff.

Lettuce should be shredded with the fingers and not cut with a knife.

Finely shredded cabbage is a useful alternative to lettuce.

Grated cheese can be kept for some time in a tightly sealed jar.

1 tablespoon or 15 g ($\frac{1}{2}$ oz.) gelatine sets approximately 500 ml (1 pint) liquid

The juice of 1 lemon = 2–3 tablespoons

GLOSSARY

ASPIC. A savoury jelly.

BAKE BLIND. To cook pastry cases without a filling. A pastry shell is usually lined with waxed paper and filled with dried peas or beans to prevent the pastry rising.

TO BASTE. To keep food moist while baking or roasting, by spooning over the liquid in which it is being cooked.

TO BLANCH. To boil for a few minutes in water. Blanching removes strong flavours and softens and tenderizes vegetables and meat before further cooking. Tomatoes are easily skinned after blanching.

BOUQUET GARNI. A bunch of mixed herbs used to give flavour to soups and sauces. The most usual combination is two sprigs of parsley, a bay leaf, and a sprig of thyme. Bouquets garnis can be bought ready made up and neatly tied in muslin. Remove before serving.

COURT BOUILLON. A mixture of water, wine and herbs in which to poach fish and shellfish. To each litre (quart) of water add: 250 ml ($\frac{1}{2}$ pint) white wine, 1 tablespoon lemon juice, 8 peppercorns, 1 teaspoon salt, a bouquet garni, 1 onion, and 1 carrot.

CROÛTONS. Small cubes of bread fried until crisp in oil, bacon fat or lard, and served with soups.

CRUDITÉS. Raw vegetables served as a first course.

TO DICE. To cut meat, vegetables or fish into small cubes.

EMULSION. A thick smooth mixture formed by adding oil slowly to an absorbent ingredient such as egg yolk or mustard.

FINES HERBES. A mixture of herbs used for flavouring egg dishes, sauces and salad dressings (usually made up of fresh chopped parsley, chives, tarragon and chervil).

TO GARNISH. To decorate dishes by adding chopped or sliced ingredients.

GRATIN or AU GRATIN. Dishes sprinkled with breadcrumbs or cheese and browned in a hot oven or under a grill.

JULIENNE. Thin matchstick strips of meat, fish or vegetables.

TO MASK. To cover completely with a sauce or jelly; usually the covering acts as a decoration to the dish.

MARINADE. A mixture of oil, wine vinegar or lemon juice, spices and herbs, used for soaking meat, fish or vegetables in order to season or tenderize.

TO PURÉE. To make into a smooth paste or smooth liquid by forcing through a fine sieve, through a food mill, by mincing or by blending in an electric liquidizer.

RAMEKIN. An individual earthenware dish used for baking.

SEASONING. Usually means salt and pepper but *can* mean any

substance which adds flavour to a dish, e.g. lemon juice or tabasco sauce.

SCUM. The matter which rises when fresh meat, fish and vegetables are cooked in boiling water.

TERRINE. A coarse pâté and also an earthenware dish with a tight fitting lid in which pâtés are cooked.

TOAST MELBA. Very thin toast wafers, made by slicing pieces of toast down the centre and then toasting the exposed bread sides which result.

WEIGHTS AND MEASURES

They are always a problem since methods of weighing and measuring vary so much from country to country. The cup measurement particularly is a difficulty as there is $\frac{1}{4}$ cup difference between English and American cups (see below).

I do use a lot of tablespoon measurements and these are based on the British Standard tablespoon which is slightly larger than the American tablespoon (but not enough to matter). If you are following the metric measurements use a metric spoon which holds 15ml.

All measures are level.

INTERNATIONAL MEASURES

Measure	U.K.	Australia	New Zealand	Canada	USA
1 pint	20 fl oz	20 fl oz	20 fl oz	20 fl oz	16 fl oz
1 cup	10 fl oz	8 fl oz	8 fl oz	8 fl oz	8 fl oz
1 tablespoon	$\frac{5}{8}$ fl oz	$\frac{1}{2}$ fl oz	$\frac{1}{2}$ fl oz	$\frac{1}{2}$ fl oz	$\frac{1}{2}$ fl oz
1 teaspoon	$\frac{1}{5}$ fl oz	$\frac{1}{8}$ fl oz	$\frac{1}{6}$ fl oz	$\frac{1}{6}$ fl oz	$\frac{1}{8}$ fl oz

OVEN TEMPERATURES

Every oven varies in temperature, even in the case of standard makes, and the following table should only be used as a rough guide. If you have any doubts about temperature settings refer to the maker's temperature chart.

If you cook by electricity always remember to allow the oven time to heat up thoroughly before you start cooking.

Description	Electric Setting	Gas Mark
Very cool	110 °C (225 °F)	$\frac{1}{4}$
	130 °C (250 °F)	$\frac{1}{2}$
Cool	140 °C (275 °F)	1
	150 °C (300 °F)	2
Very moderate	170 °C (325 °F)	3
Moderate	180 °C (350 °F)	4
Medium or	190 °C (375 °F)	5
Fairly hot	200 °C (400 °F)	6
Hot	220 °C (425 °F)	7
	230 °C (450 °F)	8
Very hot	240 °C (475 °F)	9

CHAPTER TWO

SOUPS

There are perhaps more varieties of soup than of any other dish – thick ones, thin ones, hot ones, cold ones, meat and vegetable broth, fish soups and shell-fish bisques. In France soup is served before both lunch and dinner and often the broth will be so succulent and filling it will be a meal in itself. In Italy one is astounded to see great bowls of thick minestrone being polished off before the main meal has even begun. Each country has its own particular specialities and to visit Russia without tasting the famous borsch would be as bad as leaving Provence without enjoying a bowl of onion soup.

Soups, broths, and chowders are mostly inexpensive to produce, and yet extremely nourishing. One's choice obviously depends to a large extent on the ingredients to hand, but it is important to remember that a thick brown soup is remarkably filling and should be followed by a relatively light main course. A jellied consommé, on the other hand, helps to whet the appetite and can precede some of the richer and heavier dishes. In the same way a thick cream soup should never be served before a main course containing a heavy cream sauce or a beef broth before a main course of roast beef.

The basis of all the best soups is a good fresh stock. Home made stocks are best of all but if time is short there are now a large number of concentrated stock cubes on the market which can be used successfully as the basis of a number of good soups.

Personally I very much prefer to serve soups in cups, with

handles and saucers, rather than in the traditional flat bowls, since cups are much easier to fill and hand round, and also retain heat for longer than flat dishes. Always take care to see that hot soup is almost at boiling point before it is served, and that chilled soups are really ice cold.

Garnish is important. A dusting of chopped parsley does much to enhance the flavour of a plain chicken broth and tomato soup without crisply fried croûtons is as disappointing to me as roast lamb without mint sauce.

Allow 250 ml ($\frac{1}{2}$ pint) of clear soup per person – a little less in the case of the thick, filling varieties.

STOCKS

Meat, poultry, and fish bones and trimmings, fresh vegetables, herbs and seasonings, form the basis of all stocks used in making soups, sauces and gravy. Use only fresh ingredients and remove as much fat as possible from any meat. Cut meat into small pieces, chop bones as small as possible, wash, peel and chop vegetables.

Having brought the stock to the boil, simmer as slowly as possible to extract the full flavour from the ingredients. Do not over season, more seasoning can always be added later. Skim the surface regularly during cooking. Strain stocks through muslin or a fine hair sieve, pressing the meat or vegetables to extract all the goodness. Leave in a cool place and remove every bit of fat when it has formed a hard crust over the surface of the stock. All stocks except fish stocks will keep for a few days but should be re-boiled daily during hot weather.

If, after cooking for the required length of time, the stock is not strong enough, remove the lid and continue cooking until it is reduced by almost a third.

Basic Clear Stock (for bouillon or consommé)

400 g (1 lb.) beef shin bones
400 g (1 lb.) veal knuckle
400 g (1 lb.) shin of beef
2 carrots
2 onions
1 stick celery
15 g ($\frac{1}{2}$ oz.) beef dripping
Bouquet garni (parsley, thyme, marjoram and bay leaf)
Salt
4 peppercorns
Enough water to cover (2–3 litres (4–6 quarts))

Ask your butcher to chop the bones into small pieces. Cut the meat into small pieces. Slice the carrots, peel and roughly chop the onions, chop the celery. Melt the fat in a large heavy pan. Brown the meat and vegetables quickly over a fierce heat. Add the bouquet garni, salt and peppercorns. Cover with cold water and bring to the boil. Remove all scum from the surface, partially cover and simmer over a low heat for 3 hours.

Cool, strain through muslin or a fine hair sieve and leave in a cold place. Remove all fat before using.

Basic Brown Stock

Make the day before required

800 g (2 lb.) beef bones with some meat
1 veal knuckle
25 g (1 oz.) butter or meat dripping
2 large carrots
2 large onions
2 bacon rinds
Bouquet garni (parsley, thyme, marjoram and bay leaf)
Salt
4 black peppercorns
2 litres (4 pints) cold water

Ask your butcher to chop the bones into small pieces. Trim off all the meat removing as much fat as possible. Slice the carrots. Peel the onions but leave on the inner layers of brown skin, cut into quarters. Melt the butter or dripping in a heavy pan with a close fitting lid. Brown the bones, meat and vegetables in the fat over a fierce heat. Add the bacon rinds, bouquet garni, a pinch of salt and the peppercorns. Pour over the water and bring quickly to the boil. Skim off the surface. Cover and simmer over a very low heat for 5 hours, removing any scum from the surface from time to time. Add more water as necessary.

Cool, strain through muslin or a fine hair sieve and leave in a cold place. Remove all the fat from the surface before using.

Note: Left-over soups made from meat, poultry and fresh vegetables can be added to the used bones to make a second less strong stock.

Chicken Stock

400 g (1 lb.) veal bones
400 g (1 lb.) shin beef
1 raw chicken carcass and chicken giblets
15 g ($\frac{1}{2}$ oz.) butter
2 onions
2 carrots
1 stick celery
Bouquet garni
Salt
4 peppercorns
3 litres (6 pints) water

Cut the meat into small pieces. Chop the bones as small as possible. Peel and chop the vegetables. Melt the butter in a large pan. Brown the bones and vegetables over a fierce heat. Add the bouquet garni, salt, and peppercorns, cover with the water and bring to the boil. Skim the surface to remove any scum. Cover and simmer for 3 hours.

Cool. Strain through muslin or a fine sieve and leave in a cool place. Remove all the fat before using.

Cooked Meat Stock

Although the flavour is not nearly as good as that of a stock using raw bones, a useful basic stock can be made from cooked meat bones or poultry carcasses. Add fresh chopped vegetables, a bouquet garni and seasoning and simmer gently for 1–2 hours in 1 litre (2 pints) of water for each 400 g (pound) of bones. Leftover meat soups can be used to add flavour.

For a darker stock, brown the bones and vegetables in a little fat before adding the liquid.

Fish Stock

1·25 kg (3 lbs.) fresh fish bones and trimmings (sole, plaice, whiting, brill, etc.)
2 onions
1 stick celery
1 bay leaf
3 sprigs parsley
1 sprig thyme
1 teaspoon lemon juice
Salt and 4 peppercorns
1·75 litres (3½ pints) water and 250 ml (½ pint) dry white wine

Finely chop the onions and the celery and place them in the bottom of a pan with the bay leaf, parsley, and thyme. Add the fish bones and trimmings, lemon juice, salt, and peppercorns. Pour over the water and wine.

Bring to the boil, skim, cover and simmer very gently for 30 minutes. Cool and strain through a hair sieve or a piece of muslin.

White Stock

1 kg (2½ lbs.) knuckle of veal
2 onions

1 stick celery
Bouquet garni
Salt
4 black peppercorns
3 litres (6 pints) water

Remove all the meat from the bones. Chop the meat and break the bones into small pieces. Peel and chop the vegetables and add to the meat in a large pan. Add the herbs and seasoning and cover with cold water. Bring to the boil, skim the surface. Cover and simmer for 5 hours. Cool, strain through a fine sieve and leave in a cool place.

Remove all the fat before using.

White Chicken Stock

Use 600 g (1½ lb.) of veal, a raw chicken carcass and chicken giblets. Make in the same way as white stock.

Vegetable Stock

1·25 kg (3 lb.) mixed vegetables (onions, carrots, turnips, leeks, etc.)
Bouquet garni
Salt
4 peppercorns
15g (½ oz.) butter
3 litres (6 pints) water

Peel and roughly chop the vegetables. Melt the butter in a large pan. Add the vegetables and cook over a low heat until they are soft but not brown. Add the bouquet garni, salt and peppercorns and cover with cold water. Bring to the boil, skim the surface, cover and simmer over a low flame for 3 hours.

Cool, strain through a fine sieve and leave in a cool place. Skim off all the fat before using.

MEAT, POULTRY, AND GAME SOUPS

Consommé

1 litre (2 pints) basic brown stock
200 g ($\frac{1}{2}$ lb.) raw minced shin beef
Whites and shells of 2 eggs
1 finely chopped onion
1 finely chopped carrot
1 finely chopped stick celery
Salt and pepper
2 tablespoons dry sherry

Remove all the fat from the stock. Crush the egg shells and place them in a large pan with the minced meat, vegetables and cold stock.

Whip the egg whites to a froth and add to the stock.

Heat slowly, whisking with a wire whisk, until boiling. Stop whisking and when the liquid rises to the top of the pan remove it from the heat and leave for a minute to settle. Return to a gentle heat and simmer very slowly for 30 minutes.

Strain the soup through a scalded muslin cloth. Return to the pan. Season with salt and pepper and add the sherry. Reheat and serve with freshly made hot toast.

Consommé Julienne

1 litre (2 pints) consommé
4 carrots

Peel the carrots and cut them into wafer thin matchstick strips. Cook in boiling salted water until just tender and add to the soup before serving.

Consommé à La Bourgeoise

1 litre (2 pints) consommé
1 litre (2 pints) stock
2 potatoes
4 carrots
1 small turnip
100 g ($\frac{1}{4}$ lb.) peas
4 chervil leaves or
$\frac{1}{2}$ teaspoon dried chervil

Peel the potatoes, carrots and turnip and cut them into really tiny dice. Add the vegetables and chervil to the stock. Bring the stock to the boil and cook until the vegetables are just tender. Drain the vegetables and reserve the stock to use again.

Add the cooked vegetables to the consommé just before serving.

Consommé with Mushrooms

100 g ($\frac{1}{4}$ lb.) small firm button mushrooms
1 litre (2 pints) consommé

Wash the mushrooms if necessary and dry well. Remove any tough stalks and cut them into paper thin slices. Blanch the mushrooms for 5 minutes in the gently boiling consommé before serving.

Consommé Madrilène
(chicken and tomato consommé)

400 g (1 lb.) tomatoes
1 litre (2 pints) chicken stock
200 g ($\frac{1}{2}$ lb.) minced shin beef
Whites and shells of 2 eggs
2 tablespoons dry sherry
1 slice lemon peel
1 teaspoon dried tarragon leaves, or
    $\frac{1}{2}$ teaspoon chopped fresh tarragon

Put the stock into a clean enamel pan. Add the tomatoes roughly chopped, the minced beef, egg shells and the egg whites whipped to a froth. Add the sherry and lemon peel.

Cook over a medium heat, whisking continually with a wire whisk, until the soup boils. Remove from the heat and leave for 2 minutes to settle. Return to the stove and simmer over a very low heat for 30 minutes. Leave to cool for 10 minutes and then strain through a damp cloth.

Blanch the tarragon leaves in boiling water for 2 minutes. Add to the soup, check seasoning and serve the soup hot with garlic bread (see page 227) and a thin slice of lemon floating in each bowl.

Beef Broth and Forcemeat Balls

Broth
> 400 g (1 lb.) shin beef
> 1 onion
> 1 carrot
> 1 turnip
> 25 g (1 oz.) butter or dripping
> 25 g (1 oz.) flour
> 1 litre (2 pints) brown stock
> Salt and freshly ground black pepper
> 2 teaspoons Worcester sauce
> Chopped parsley

Forcemeat Balls
> 1 tablespoon fresh white breadcrumbs
> ½ tablespoon chopped suet
> 1 teaspoon mixed herbs
> 1 egg
> A pinch of nutmeg
> A little grated lemon peel
> Salt and cayenne pepper

Remove any fat from the meat. Cut or mince finely. Peel and chop the vegetables.

Melt the butter in a heavy pan. Add the onion and cook

over a medium heat until golden brown. Add the flour, mix well and allow to brown.

Add the vegetables, meat and stock. Bring to the boil, season with salt, pepper, and Worcester sauce. Cover and simmer for 1½ hours. Strain.

TO MAKE THE FORCEMEAT BALLS. Mix all the ingredients except the egg in a basin. Add the beaten egg and mix to a smooth paste. Form into 8 small balls.

Heat the strained soup to boiling point. Add the forcemeat balls and simmer for ½ hour.

Serve with a garnish of chopped parsley.

Borsch

A beetroot-flavoured soup from Russia and Poland. It should be made with stock from a wild or domestic duck but a strong beef stock will do.

50 g (2 oz.) chopped streaky bacon
1 sliced leek
1 chopped onion
2 peeled and chopped raw beetroots
½ small shredded cabbage
1½ tablespoons tomato purée
750 ml (1½ pints) strong stock
500 ml (1 pint) water
Salt and pepper
Juice of ½ lemon
Sour cream

Fry the bacon in a heavy pan without extra fat, for three minutes. Add the leek and onion and cook over a medium heat until golden. Add the beetroot, cabbage, tomato purée, stock and water. Season with salt and pepper.

Bring to the boil, cover and simmer for one hour. Strain, add lemon juice, check seasoning and serve hot with a spoonful of sour cream floating on the top of each bowl.

Note: Use rubber gloves when peeling and chopping beetroot.

Mulligatawny

This is a thick rich curry flavoured brown soup. Good for a cold winter night but too filling to be followed by a rich or heavy main course.

1 litre (2 pints) strong beef stock
8 g (¼ oz.) cardamom seeds
6 black peppercorns
8 g (¼ oz.) cumin seed   }*
8 g (¼ oz.) fenugreek
1 bay leaf
(*or 2 teaspoons curry paste)
Thinly pared rind of ½ lemon
2 tablespoons desiccated coconut
1 onion or 2 shallots chopped
25 g (1 oz.) butter
25 g (1 oz.) flour
1 teaspoon curry powder
Salt and pepper

Crush the spices with a wooden spoon. Tie them in a muslin bag with the bay leaf and lemon peel. Add the spices to the stock and simmer over a low flame for half an hour. Remove the spices. Steep the coconut in 125 ml (¼ pint) of boiling water for half an hour.

Melt the butter in a heavy saucepan. Add the onion and cook over a medium flame until the onion is transparent. Add the curry powder, mix well and continue to cook for 3 minutes. Add the flour, mix well and gradually add the stock, stirring continually until the liquid is thickened and smooth.

Simmer the soup for 15 minutes. Add the strained milk from the coconut. Season with salt and pepper. Serve hot.

Scotch Broth

600 g (1½ lbs.) neck of mutton
1·5 litres (3 pints) cold water
40 g (1½ oz.) pearl barley soaked overnight
1 carrot

3 leeks or 1 large onion
1 turnip
Salt and freshly ground black pepper
1 tablespoon chopped parsley

Ask your butcher to chop the mutton into small pieces.
Remove as much fat as possible. Put the mutton into the
water in a large saucepan. Bring slowly to the boil, skimming
the surface of all scum that rises. Add the barley, season well
with salt. Cover and simmer for 30 minutes. Cut the vegetables into small dice. Add them to the soup and continue to
simmer for 1½ hours until the meat is tender.

Remove the bones and cut the meat into small pieces.
Return them to the soup with the parsley. Skim off any fat
from the surface and season with freshly ground black pepper.
Heat through before serving.

Oxtail Soup

1 oxtail
25g (1 oz.) butter or bacon fat
1 onion
2 carrots
1 small turnip
1 stick celery
3 litres (6 pints) stock
Bouquet garni
4 black peppercorns
¼ teaspoon salt
200 g (½ lb.) shin beef, minced
Whites and shells of 2 eggs
2 tablespoons sherry

Ask your butcher to cut the oxtail into joints. Roughly chop
the onions, carrots, turnip and celery.

Melt the fat in a heavy pan. Add the vegetables. Cook over
a medium heat for 5 minutes. Add the oxtail and continue to
cook until the meat and vegetables are lightly browned.

Add the stock, bouquet garni, and peppercorns and salt.

Bring slowly to the boil, skimming the surface as any scum rises. Cover the stock and simmer for 1½–2 hours. Reserve the pieces of oxtail. Leave the stock to get cold and remove all the fat from the surface.

Put 1 litre (2 pints) of the stock in a clean enamel pan with the sherry, minced beef, crushed egg shells and the egg whites whipped to a froth. Bring slowly to the boil whisking continually with a wire whisk until the soup rises to the top of the pan. Remove from the heat and leave for a minute to settle. Return to a gentle heat and simmer very slowly for 30 minutes.

Strain the stock through a clean damp cloth. Return the stock to the pan and add the oxtail meat removed from the bone. Reheat, check seasoning and add more sherry if necessary.

Ham and Celery Soup

1 head of celery
1 onion
50 g (2 oz.) butter
750 ml (1½ pints) milk
2 blades of mace
1 bay leaf
25 g (1 oz.) flour
Salt and freshly ground black pepper
2 egg yolks
2 tablespoons cream
100 g (4 oz.) smoked ham, chopped
Chopped parsley

Discard the leaves of the celery but keep the base of the stem. Slice the celery and the onion finely.

Melt 25 g (1 oz.) of the butter in a heavy saucepan. Add the onion and celery. Cook over a low heat for 20 minutes until the vegetables are really tender. Purée through a fine sieve, a food mill or an electric blender.

Heat the milk with the mace and the bay leaf. Bring slowly to the boil and simmer for 5 minutes. Strain and cool. Melt the remaining butter in a saucepan. Add the flour and mix well. Gradually add the milk, stirring continually until the mixture is smooth. Bring to the boil and simmer for 5 minutes. Blend the hot liquid with the purée, a little at a time. Return to the saucepan and season with salt and freshly ground black pepper. Beat the egg yolks with the cream and add to the hot soup. Reheat but do not boil. Add the finely chopped ham and garnish with a little chopped parsley. Serve hot.

Cream of Chicken Soup

500 ml (1 pint) chicken stock and 1 chicken stock cube
500 ml (1 pint) milk
40 g (1½ oz.) butter
40 g (1½ oz.) flour
50–100 g (2–4 oz.) cooked chicken
Salt and pepper
1 tablespoon chopped chervil
1 egg yolk
125 ml (¼ pint) cream
Chopped parsley

Melt the butter in a saucepan. Add the flour and mix well. Gradually add the stock and milk, stirring continually over a moderate heat until the soup is thick and smooth. Add the chopped chicken, chicken stock cube, seasoning and chervil. Cover and simmer for 10 minutes. Mix the egg yolk with the cream. Remove the soup from the heat and stir in the egg-cream mixture. Reheat but do not boil.

Serve hot with a garnish of chopped parsley.

Chicken Giblet Soup

It is usually possible to buy chicken giblets from a butcher or poulterer and I have noticed recently that more and more large supermarkets are selling packs of frozen chicken giblets which are ideal for making this nourishing and well flavoured soup.

The giblets of 2 chickens (livers, gizzards, necks and
  hearts)
50 g (2 oz.) bacon fat or butter
1 small chopped onion
25 g (1 oz.) flour
1·25 litres (2½ pints) water
Bouquet garni
Salt and pepper
2 tablespoons sherry
Chopped parsley

Melt the fat or butter in a heavy pan. Add the chopped onion
and cook over a low heat until transparent. Add the flour, mix
well and cook for 3 minutes. Gradually add the water, stirring
continually. Add the giblets and the bouquet garni. Season
with salt and pepper. Cover and simmer for 2 hours or until
the gizzards are really tender.

Strain the soup and skim any fat from the surface. Remove
the skin from the gizzards. Chop them and the liver into very
small pieces. Add to the soup. Reheat, add the sherry and
serve hot with a garnish of chopped parsley.

Note: This soup can be made with duck, goose or turkey
giblets.

Cock-A-Leekie Soup

1 small boiling fowl
Salt and pepper
6 leeks
75 g (3 oz.) butter
2·25 litres (4½ pints) stock or water
2 sprigs of parsley and 1 of thyme
50 g (2 oz.) rice

Cut the fowl into 6 pieces. Season with salt and pepper.
Carefully clean and slice the leeks. Melt the butter in a large
saucepan. Add the fowl and sauté on all sides until a golden

brown. Add the leeks and continue to cook on a low heat until they turn transparent. Pour over the stock or water. Add the parsley and thyme, bring to the boil, skim off the surface and simmer for 1¼ hours.

Add the rice and continue to simmer for a further ¾ hour or until the fowl is really tender. Remove the pieces of fowl and the herbs. Chop the meat and return to the soup. Check seasoning and serve hot.

Note: This soup is improved by being made the day before it is required. It can then be left to settle and any fat removed from the surface.

VEGETABLE SOUPS

Cabbage Soup

This is a cheap and nourishing soup, very good to serve on winter evenings.

1 large cabbage
25 g (1 oz.) butter
25 g (1 oz.) flour
1 litre (2 pints) chicken stock
Salt and pepper
8 small frankfurters or 8 thin slices garlic sausage

Cut the hard core and stalks from the cabbage and shred the leaves. Melt the butter in a heavy pan. Add the cabbage and cook it gently until transparent. Add the flour and mix well. Gradually blend in the stock, stirring continually. Bring to the boil, season with salt and pepper. Cover and simmer for 1 hour.

Boil the frankfurters and cut them into thin slices. Skim the surface of the soup, add the frankfurters or slices of garlic sausage and serve hot, with rye bread.

Cauliflower and Tomato Soup

1 cauliflower
800 g (2 lb.) chopped ripe tomatoes
1 litre (2 pints) chicken stock
1 large sliced onion
1 teaspoon vinegar
25 g (1 oz.) butter
Sugar, salt and freshly ground black pepper
2 tablespoons cream

Wash and trim the cauliflower keeping as much of the greenery as possible. Boil in salted water until tender, 20–30 minutes. Drain well and mash until smooth.

Melt the butter in a heavy pan. Add the onion and cook over a moderate heat until transparent. Add the tomatoes and continue to cook for 5 minutes. Add the cauliflower, vinegar, and stock. Season with sugar, salt and pepper to taste and stir well. Bring to the boil, then simmer for a further 20 minutes. Rub through a hair sieve or food mill, or purée in an electric liquidizer.

Stir in the cream, check seasoning. Reheat but do not boil.

Leek and Potato Soup

This is a great favourite of mine, when leeks are cheap and plentiful. Be careful as they are the dirtiest of all vegetables. Soak them well in salted water to avoid gritty soup.

6 leeks
3 large potatoes
50 g (2 oz.) butter
1·25 litres (2½ pints) stock
Grated cheese
Salt and freshly ground black pepper

Take off the tough green leaves of the leeks and wash the rest carefully. Cut into thin slices. Peel and dice the potatoes.

Melt the butter in a heavy pan. Add the leeks and potatoes and cook over a medium heat until golden but not burnt, about 6 minutes. Pour over the stock, bring to the boil, skim the surface, season with salt and pepper and simmer for 20–30 minutes until the vegetables are tender.

Serve with grated cheese.

Note: The soup can be made with water in the place of stock and put through a sieve or food mill before serving.

Watercress and Leek Soup

    2 large potatoes
    2 leeks
    1 bunch watercress
    50 g (2 oz.) butter
    1 litre (2 pints) chicken stock
    1 egg yolk
    1 tablespoon milk or single cream
    Salt and pepper

Peel and cut the potatoes into very small dice. Carefully clean and slice the leeks. Chop the watercress, keeping a little for the garnish.

Melt the butter in a heavy pan. Add the vegetables and cook over a medium flame, without browning, for 4 minutes. Add the stock and season with salt and pepper. Bring to the boil and simmer for 20 minutes, until the potatoes are soft.

Beat the egg yolk with the milk or cream and stir into the soup before serving. Do not reboil. Garnish with a little chopped watercress.

Hot Lettuce Soup

This is a perfect first course for chilly summer evenings.

    2 shredded round cabbage lettuces
    2 chopped shallots or 4 chopped spring onions
    40 g (1½ oz.) butter
    750 ml (1½ pints) chicken stock or water and chicken stock
        cubes
    250 ml (½ pint) cream
    Salt and pepper and ½ teaspoon sugar

Melt the butter in a heavy saucepan. Add the lettuce and shallots. Cook over a low heat for 5 minutes until the vegetables are transparent but not browned.

Bring the stock to boiling point and add the lettuce and shallots. Season with salt, pepper and sugar. Cover and simmer for 15 minutes. Put through a fine sieve or a food mill, or blend in an electric liquidizer.

Return the soup to the pan. Blend in the cream. Reheat but *do not boil*. Check seasoning and serve hot, garnished with croûtons of crisply fried bread.

French Onion Soup

6 medium onions
25 g (1 oz.) butter
1 litre (2 pints) brown stock
8 slices dry French bread
100 g (¼ lb.) grated Gruyère cheese
Salt and freshly ground black pepper

Peel the onions and cut them into thin slices. Melt the butter in a heavy pan. Add the onions and cook over a medium flame until they are golden brown. Stir to prevent burning.

Add the stock and bring to the boil. Simmer uncovered for 20–30 minutes. Season with salt and plenty of freshly ground black pepper.

Pour the soup into individual earthenware or ovenproof dishes. Float 2 pieces of bread, well covered with grated cheese, in each bowl and brown the surface under a hot grill or in a hot oven (230 C., 450 F., Reg. 8).

Swedish Pea Soup with Pork

This soup is traditionally served on Thursdays in Sweden. It is very, very filling and should be followed by the lightest of main courses. In fact, for most people, fresh fruit and cheese would be ample.

400 g (1 lb.) split yellow peas
2 litres (4 pints) water
300 g ($\frac{3}{4}$ lb.) lightly salted pork
2 sliced medium onions
$\frac{1}{2}$ teaspoon ginger
1 teaspoon marjoram
Salt and pepper
Mustard

Rinse the peas in cold running water. Cover with the 2 litres (4 pints) water in a large saucepan and leave to soak overnight.

Cover the saucepan and bring quickly to the boil. Remove any shells floating on the surface. Simmer for 2 hours. Add the pork, onions, ginger and marjoram. Cover and simmer for a further hour. Season with salt and pepper.

Remove the pork, cut it into slices and serve it separately with mustard.

Dried Pea or Lentil Soup

200 g ($\frac{1}{2}$ lb.) dried peas or lentils
1·5 litres (3 pints) chicken stock
1 lemon
Salt and freshly ground black pepper

Soak the peas or lentils in 1 litre (2 pints) of water for 12 hours (or overnight). Drain well. Cook the soaked peas or lentils in the stock for 1$\frac{1}{2}$ hours until they are tender. Rub them through a fine sieve or a food mill, or blend in an electric liquidizer. Reheat and season with salt and freshly ground black pepper. Thin with more stock or water if necessary.

Serve with a thin slice of lemon floating on each bowl and with crisply fried bread croûtons served separately.

Dried Mushroom Soup

Packets of dried mushrooms can be bought from most good delicatessen stores. They have a strong, almost meaty, flavour and, apart from being a useful addition to stews and casseroles, make a good soup.

25 g (1 oz.) packet dried mushrooms
2 carrots
1 onion
Bouquet garni
Salt and pepper

Soak the dried mushrooms in 500 ml (1 pint) warm water for 3 hours. Drain and cut into thin strips. Roughly chop the carrots and onion. Add to the mushrooms, their liquid, bouquet garni and 750 ml (1½ pints) water. Bring to the boil and simmer for 1 hour over a low heat.

Strain the soup. Discard the onion, carrot and bouquet garni. Return the mushrooms to the stock and reheat. Season with salt and pepper.

Sweetcorn Chowder

Another rich and filling soup. This is a particular favourite with children and makes a good supper dish that can be followed by fresh fruit.

3 rashers chopped bacon
25 g (1 oz.) butter
1 chopped onion
2 chopped celery sticks
1 chopped green pepper
2 peeled and diced medium potatoes
500 ml (1 pint) water
1 small bay leaf
Salt and pepper
2 tablespoons flour
500 ml (1 pint) milk
1 tin sweetcorn
Parsley

Melt the butter in a heavy saucepan. Add the bacon and cook for 3 minutes over a medium flame. Add the onion, celery and green pepper. Cook for 5 minutes until the vegetables are golden brown.

Add the potatoes, the water and the bay leaf. Season with salt and pepper. Bring to the boil and simmer for 25 minutes or until the potatoes are tender.

Make a paste with the flour and 125 ml ($\frac{1}{4}$ pint) milk. Add to the soup slowly, stirring continually. Bring the soup to the boil and add the rest of the milk and the sweetcorn. Heat but do not reboil.

Check seasoning and serve hot with a garnish of chopped parsley.

Tomato Soup à L'Estragon

1 onion
400 g (1 lb.) ripe tomatoes
15 g ($\frac{1}{2}$ oz.) butter
1 clove garlic
Salt
Sugar
2 teaspoons tomato purée
250 ml ($\frac{1}{2}$ pint) tinned tomato juice
750 ml (1$\frac{1}{2}$ pints) strong beef stock
1 bay leaf
2 teaspoons arrowroot
2 tablespoons chopped tarragon

Slice the onion and roughly chop the tomatoes. Melt the butter in a heavy pan, add the tomatoes, onions and crushed garlic. Season with salt and a pinch of sugar. Cook over a very low flame for 30 minutes. Rub through a fine sieve.

Combine the sieved tomatoes, tomato purée, tomato juice, stock and bay leaf in a saucepan and simmer for 20 minutes.

Mix the arrowroot to a thin paste with a little of the soup. Add to the soup with the tarragon leaves. Bring to the boil, stirring continually. Check seasoning.

The soup can be served hot or cold with hot cheese paprika biscuits or cheese straws.

Spring Vegetable Soup

4 carrots
100 g (¼ lb.) peas
6 spring onions
1 tablespoon bacon fat
1 litre (2 pints) chicken stock
Salt and pepper
½ teaspoon chopped chervil

Wash the carrots and cut them into tiny dice. Clean the spring onions and cut them into thin slices. Melt the fat in a heavy pan. Add the onions and carrots and cook over a medium heat until the onions are transparent. Drain off any excess fat.

Add the stock and the peas. Cover and simmer for 15–20 minutes until the vegetables are tender but still firm. Season with salt and pepper and chopped chervil.

Minestrone (Italian vegetable soup)

The vegetables can be varied according to the season.

1·5 litres (3 pints) brown stock
2 sticks tender celery with leaves
2 carrots cut into thin slices
100 g (4 oz.) finely chopped bacon
200 g (8 oz.) skinned and chopped tomatoes
1 thinly sliced small onion
100 g (4 oz.) spaghetti
Salt and pepper
100 g (4 oz.) grated cheese

Bring the stock to the boil. Add the celery, carrots and bacon and simmer for 30 minutes. Add the remaining vegetables and the spaghetti. Season with salt and pepper and simmer for a further 30 minutes.

Serve hot with 25 g (1 oz.) grated cheese sprinkled over each serving.

Note: I break up my spaghetti before adding it to the soup. This is not strictly correct but makes it much easier to cope with.

Julienne Soup (*French vegetable soup*)

2 potatoes
2 carrots
2 small turnips
2 leeks
1 small onion
4 cabbage leaves
50 g (2 oz.) butter
1·25 litres (2½ pints) vegetable or chicken stock
100 g (¼ lb.) green peas, fresh or frozen
Salt and pepper

Clean the vegetables and cut into thin matchstick strips.

Melt the butter in a heavy pan. Add all the vegetables except for the peas. Cook over a medium flame for 4–5 minutes without burning.

Add the stock and the peas and bring to the boil. Cover and simmer for 15 minutes (a little less if the peas are frozen). Season with salt and pepper.

CREAM SOUPS

Care should be taken to make sure the soup is completely smooth and not too thick; if necessary strain it before serving. Cream soups should never be boiled and should be well seasoned

Use chicken stock, a white stock or milk with a bouillon cube dissolved in it. Brown stock gives the soup an unattractive appearance.

Garnish cream soups with chopped lettuce, chopped parsley, fried bread croûtons or finely chopped, crisply fried bacon.

Remember that cream soups are filling and should be followed by a light main course and never by one that is served with a white or cream sauce.

Cream of Asparagus Soup

Personally I cannot understand why anyone would want to eat fresh asparagus in any form besides its natural state. Therefore I am giving a recipe that uses tinned asparagus instead of the fresh. It is of course inferior to the real thing but greatly superior to tinned asparagus soup.

> 2 tins whole asparagus spears
> 500 ml (1 pint) chicken or white stock
> 1 chopped medium onion
> 1 chopped celery stick
> 25 g (1 oz.) butter
> 25 g (1 oz.) flour
> 3 tablespoons cream
> Salt and paprika pepper

Drain the asparagus and reserve the juice. Cut off the tips and keep them on one side. Chop the stalks, and place them in a saucepan with the onion, celery, stock and asparagus juice. Bring to the boil and simmer for 20 minutes. Rub the vegetables through a fine sieve. Melt the butter in a clean pan, add the flour and stir until blended, gradually mix in the stock and vegetable purée, stirring continually until the soup is thick and smooth. Season with salt and paprika and stir in the asparagus tips and the cream before serving. Heat through but do not boil.

Note: If the soup is too thick add a little milk or thin cream.

Cream of Carrot Soup

A delicate orange coloured soup, cheap to make and pretty to look at.

> 50 g (2 oz.) butter
> 600 g (1½ lbs.) sliced carrots
> 200 g (½ lb.) quartered tomatoes
> 750 ml (1½ pints) chicken stock
> 125 ml (¼ pint) milk
> 125 ml (¼ pint) single cream

½ teaspoon chervil
Salt and pepper
1 tablespoon chopped parsley

Melt the butter in a heavy saucepan. Add the carrots. Cook over a low heat for 3 minutes. Add the tomatoes and cook for a further 3 minutes.

Heat the stock. Add to the carrots and tomatoes with the chervil. Season with salt and pepper. Cover and simmer for 30 minutes until the carrots are tender. Rub through a fine sieve, a food mill, or blend in an electric liquidizer.

Return the purée to the pan. Add the milk and the cream. Heat but do not boil. Adjust seasoning. Serve hot with a garnish of chopped parsley and fried bread croûtons.

Cream Duchess Soup

A bland creamy soup well flavoured with cheese. Good before a highly spiced main course.

25 g (1 oz.) butter
1 small finely chopped onion
15 g (½ oz.) flour
750 ml (1½ pints) milk
50 g (2 oz.) grated Gruyère cheese
2 egg yolks
250 ml (½ pint) cream
Salt and paprika pepper
A small pinch of celery salt
A small pinch of cayenne pepper
1 lemon

Melt the butter in a heavy saucepan. Add the onion and cook over a low flame until the onion is transparent. Do not brown. Add the flour and mix well. Gradually blend in the milk, stirring continually until the soup is smooth. Cook slowly for 10 minutes or until the onion is soft. Strain through a sieve and reheat.

Beat the egg yolks with the cream. Add the grated cheese and mix well. Add to the soup. Stir well. Do not allow to boil.

Season with salt, paprika pepper and a very little celery salt and cayenne.

Serve with a thin slice of lemon floating in each bowl.

Cream of Cucumber Soup

Hot cucumber soup is unusual. It has a delicate flavour and is suitable to serve before a rich meat course.

2 medium cucumbers
625 ml (1¼ pints) chicken or white stock
25 g (1 oz.) butter
1 tablespoon flour
125 ml (¼ pint) milk
Salt and pepper
125 ml (¼ pint) cream
1 lemon

Peel the cucumbers, remove the seeds and cut into pieces. Blanch in boiling salted water for 3 minutes. Drain well.

Bring the stock to the boil, then add the cucumber. Simmer for 20 minutes, or until the cucumber is tender. Purée through a fine sieve, a food mill or in an electric liquidizer.

Melt the butter in a saucepan, add the flour and mix well. Gradually add the purée, stirring continually until the mixture is thick and smooth. Blend in the milk. Season with salt and pepper. Add the cream and heat through. Do not boil.

Serve with a thin slice of lemon floating in each serving and with crisply fried bread croûtons served separately.

Cream of Mushroom Soup

200 g (½ lb.) firm mushrooms
1½ teaspoons mushroom ketchup
Bouquet garni
750 ml (1½ pints) water
40 g (1½ oz.) butter
50 g (2 oz.) flour
250 ml (½ pint) milk
Salt and pepper

Wash the mushrooms but do not peel them. Cover with the water and add the mushroom ketchup, and bouquet garni. Bring slowly to the boil and simmer for 20 minutes. Remove the bouquet garni and rub the mushrooms through a fine sieve or food mill, or purée in an electric liquidizer.

Melt the butter in a saucepan. Add the flour and mix well. Gradually add the milk, stirring continually until the mixture is smooth and thick. Add the mushroom purée and liquid. Season with salt and pepper.

Serve hot with croûtons of crisply fried bread.

Note: A few thinly sliced raw mushrooms can be used as a garnish.

Cream of Onion Soup

2 large onions
25 g (1 oz.) butter
15g ($\frac{1}{2}$ oz.) flour
750 ml (1$\frac{1}{2}$ pints) hot milk
2 tablespoons cream
2 egg yolks
Salt, pepper and nutmeg

Peel the onions and cut them into wafer-thin slices. Melt the butter in a heavy pan. Add the onions and cook over a low heat until they are soft and transparent. Add the flour. Cook over a low flame for 3 minutes stirring continually. Do not brown.

Gradually add the hot milk, a little at a time, stirring continually until the soup is smooth and has the consistency of thin cream. Bring to the boil and simmer until the onions are very tender – 10–15 minutes. Remove from the heat.

Beat the egg yolks with the cream. Add to the soup and stir well. Season with salt, pepper and a pinch of grated nutmeg. Do not boil.

Serve hot poured over rounds of toasted bread.

Cream of Pea Soup

1 chopped shallot or 3 chopped spring onions
½ shredded lettuce
600 g (1½ lbs.) shelled peas or 1·25 kg (3 lbs.) unshelled
   peas
15 g (½ oz.) butter
125 ml (¼ pint) milk
125 ml (¼ pint) cream
Salt, pepper and ½ teaspoon sugar

Melt the butter in a saucepan. Add the shallot and the lettuce. Cook over a low heat until the shallot is transparent but not browned. Add the peas, cover with water and season with the salt, pepper and sugar. Simmer for 20 minutes. Drain and reserve 125 ml (¼ pint) of the cooking liquid.

Put the vegetables through a fine sieve or food mill, or blend in an electric liquidizer. Return the purée to the pan. Blend in the 125 ml (¼ pint) cooking liquid and the milk. Heat through and add the cream. Do not boil. Check seasoning.

This soup can be served hot or cold. Garnish with a little shredded lettuce and serve with hot garlic bread (see page 227).

Pumpkin Soup

It's a pity that more people don't grow pumpkins. They are easy to cultivate and form the basis for many vegetable dishes, including this good winter soup.

400 g (1 lb.) pumpkin
1 sliced onion
1·5 litres (3 pints) salted water
375 ml (¾ pint) milk
2 tablespoons cream
Salt and freshly ground black pepper
2 eggs
15 g (½ oz.) butter

Peel the pumpkin and cut it into pieces. Put it in a heavy saucepan together with the onion and the water. Cover and boil for 15 minutes or until the pumpkin is soft.

Drain and reserve the liquid and put the pumpkin through a fine sieve or food mill, or blend in an electric liquidizer.

Put the puréed pumpkin in the top of a double saucepan. Stir in the milk and cream. The soup should have the consistency of thin cream. If it is too thick, thin it with a little of the vegetable water. Season with salt and pepper and cook over simmering water for 20 minutes.

Beat the eggs. Add 2 tablespoons of the soup and mix well. Gradually add the egg mixture to the soup stirring constantly until it is smooth and slightly thickened. Check seasoning. Stir in the butter and serve at once.

Potato Soup

3 large potatoes
2 large onions
4 sticks celery
25 g (1 oz.) butter
750 ml (1½ pints) white stock or chicken stock
1 tablespoon cream
Salt and pepper
1 tablespoon finely chopped parsley

Peel and slice the potatoes. Skin and chop the onions. Clean and chop the celery.

Place the vegetables in a saucepan. Cover with boiling water and cook for 30 minutes or until the vegetables are tender. Drain well and rub through a fine sieve. Blend in the butter and slowly stir in the stock. Season with salt and pepper. Reheat but do not boil. Stir in the cream and chopped parsley just before serving.

Cream of Spinach Soup

800 g (2 lbs.) spinach or 1 large packet frozen spinach
1 tablespoon grated or finely chopped onion
25 g (1 oz.) butter
25 g (1 oz.) flour
250 ml ($\frac{1}{2}$ pint) stock
250 ml ($\frac{1}{2}$ pint) milk
Salt
Grated nutmeg
2 tablespoons grated cheese

Pick over and wash the spinach. Cook it in boiling water until tender. Drain and rub through a fine sieve.

Melt the butter in a saucepan. Add the onion and cook over a medium heat until it turns transparent. Add the flour and stir until blended. Gradually add the stock and milk stirring continually until smooth. Add the spinach and season with salt and a little grated nutmeg.

Serve hot with grated cheese sprinkled over the surface of the soup.

Cream of Spring Vegetable Soup

2 chopped spring onions
1 stick chopped celery
2 chopped new carrots
1 small cauliflower
200 g ($\frac{1}{2}$ lb.) peas
200 g ($\frac{1}{2}$ lb.) spinach
15 g ($\frac{1}{2}$ oz.) butter
25 g (1 oz.) flour
1 litre (2 pints) chicken stock
2 egg yolks
125 ml ($\frac{1}{4}$ pint) cream
Salt and pepper
Chopped parsley

Cook the onions, celery, carrots, the cauliflower divided into small florets, and the peas, in boiling salted water until tender, about 20 minutes. Drain well. Cook the spinach separately in boiling salted water for 15 minutes. Drain and chop.

Melt the butter in a saucepan. Add the flour and mix well. Gradually add the stock, stirring continually, until the mixture is smooth. Add the vegetables. Season with salt and pepper.

Beat the egg yolks with the cream. Add 2 tablespoons of hot soup and mix well. Add to the soup. Stir and check seasoning. *Do not re-boil.* Garnish with chopped parsley and serve hot.

Cream of Tomato Soup

400 g (1 lb.) roughly chopped tomatoes
750 ml (1½ pints) chicken stock or water with 2 chicken cubes
1 chopped shallot
1 rasher chopped streaky bacon
Bouquet garni
The grated rind of 1 orange
15 g (½ oz.) butter
Salt and pepper and ½ teaspoon castor sugar
¼ teaspoon sage
250 ml (½ pint) cream

Melt the butter in a heavy saucepan. Add the shallot and bacon. Cook over a low flame for 5 minutes. Add the tomatoes, the sugar and bouquet garni. Cook for a further 3 minutes. Add the grated orange rind and the sage and season with salt and pepper. Pour over the stock. Cover and simmer for 30 minutes.

Purée through a fine sieve or food mill, or blend in an electric liquidizer. Reheat. Adjust seasoning and add cream. Do not boil. Serve with toasted cheese squares and croûtons of crisply fried bread.

FISH SOUPS

Prawn Chowder

50 g (2 oz.) butter
3 stalks celery
1 onion
½ green pepper
750 ml (1½ pints) chicken stock
1 225g (8oz.) tin tomatoes
1 bay leaf
Salt, pepper, and paprika pepper
200 g (½ lb.) peeled prawns
1 small packet frozen peas

Finely chop the celery. Peel and chop the onion. Seed, core and chop the pepper. Melt the butter in a saucepan. Add the celery, onion and pepper and cook over a medium heat until the onion is transparent. Add the chicken stock, tomatoes and bay leaf. Season with salt, pepper and paprika. Cover and simmer for 20 minutes.

Add the prawns and peas. Mix well. Cook for a further 10 minutes. Serve hot.

White Fish Soup

400 g (1 lb.) fish fillets (plaice, cod or any white fish)
2 leeks
2 medium potatoes
1 celery stalk
25 g (1 oz.) butter
¼ teaspoon mixed spice (nutmeg, pepper, allspice, cloves)
1 litre (2 pints) water or fish stock
Salt
Chopped dill, parsley or chives

Clean the leeks, remove the tough green tops and cut the rest into very thin slices. Peel the potatoes and cut into really small dice. Cut the celery into really small dice. Melt the butter in a heavy saucepan. Add the vegetables and fry gently until the leeks are soft and transparent – do not allow to brown. Add the mixed spice and pour over the water. Season with salt. Bring to the boil, and cook for 10 minutes.

Cut the fish into small dice and add to the soup. Continue to cook for a further 10 minutes or until the vegetables are tender. Sprinkle the soup with chopped dill, parsley or chives before serving.

Mock Bouillabaisse

I call this soup 'mock' as it is practically impossible to make true bouillabaisse away from the Mediterranean. It is very difficult to get the many varieties of fish and herbs needed for the real thing, which anyway is really too rich and filling to serve except as a main course. Even this soup is very filling and should only be served before a light main course.

1 carrot
2 onions
2 cloves garlic
4 tablespoons olive oil
3 tomatoes
800 g (2lbs.) haddock
1 bay leaf
500 ml (1 pint) fish stock
8 scallops
100 g ($\frac{1}{4}$ lb.) peeled prawns
Juice of $\frac{1}{2}$ lemon
Salt
Freshly ground black pepper
2 tablespoons dry sherry

Peel and chop the carrot and onions. Mince the garlic. Heat the oil in a saucepan. Add the carrot, onions and garlic. Cook over a high heat until the onions are golden brown.

Peel and chop the tomatoes. Cut the fish and scallops into 2·5 cm (1 inch) pieces. Add the tomatoes, fish and scallops to the vegetables. Pour over the fish stock and add the bay leaf.

Bring to the boil, cover and simmer for 15 minutes. Remove the bay leaf and add the prawns and lemon juice. Season with plenty of salt and pepper.

Cook for a further 5 minutes. Add the sherry and serve at once.

CHAPTER THREE

ICED SOUPS

Iced Avocado Soup

An unusual way to serve avocado pears; this soup has a subtle flavour and a smooth, bland texture.

2 ripe avocados
2 teaspoons lemon juice
750 ml (1½ pints) strong chicken stock – I use stock cubes
3 chopped spring onion bulbs
250 ml (½ pint) cream
Salt and white pepper
Chopped olives or watercress

Peel the avocados, remove stones and purée them with the lemon juice through a fine sieve or food mill, or in an electric liquidizer. Mix the avocado purée with the stock. Add the chopped onions. Heat gently in a double boiler. Blend in the cream stirring continually until the mixture is smooth. Cook over simmering water for 15 minutes.

Season with salt and pepper. Strain and chill. Serve with a garnish of chopped olives or watercress.

Iced Borsch

2 litres (4 pints) strong beef stock
800 g (2 lbs.) uncooked beetroot
2 carrots
1 onion
2 teaspoons white wine vinegar

Salt and white pepper
4 tablespoons sour cream
1 tablespoon chopped chives

Peel the beetroot and chop them in small pieces. Chop the carrots and onions. Simmer the vegetables in the stock until they are tender and the soup is a deep red. Strain gently through a fine sieve. Add the vinegar and season if necessary with salt and pepper. Serve well chilled with a tablespoonful of sour cream and chopped chives in each bowl.

Note: 2 tablespoons of chopped ham can be substituted for the cream and chives.

Jellied Consommé

750 ml (1½ pints) consommé or 2 tins consommé
15 g (½ oz.) gelatine if necessary
Juice of ½ lemon
1 tablespoon sherry
1 lemon

Make sure that the stock is well jellied. If it is not melt 15 g (½ oz.) gelatine in a little of the consommé. Combine the consommé, lemon juice and sherry. Mix well and leave in a refrigerator until set. Break up roughly with a fork and pile into soup cups.

Garnish with a quarter of lemon and serve with hot toast or hot salted biscuits.

Note: Most tinned consommés jell easily and will not need added gelatine. I find that Crosse & Blackwell make the best.

Iced Cucumber Jelly Soup

2 large cucumbers
½ small onion
½ tablespoon lemon juice
Salt and freshly ground black pepper
1 teaspoon finely chopped mint
250 ml (½ pint) aspic jelly
50 g (2 oz.) prawns

Grate the cucumber with its peel. Grate the onion and mix it with the cucumber. Season with the lemon juice, salt and freshly ground black pepper. Mix with the aspic jelly and the chopped mint. Pour into 4 dishes and leave to set. Garnish with prawns.

Serve chilled with hot garlic bread (see page 227).

Iced Cucumber Soup with Mint

2 large cucumbers
4 spring onions
250 ml ($\frac{1}{2}$ pint) sour cream
1$\frac{1}{2}$ tablespoons chopped mint
Salt and pepper

Peel the cucumbers, rub them through a sieve or food mill, or purée them in an electric liquidizer. Chop the white and green part of the spring onions very finely, and add them to the puréed cucumber with the sour cream. Add the mint. Mix well and season with salt and pepper. Serve well chilled, in soup cups.

Note: 250 ml ($\frac{1}{2}$ pint) cream and the juice of $\frac{1}{2}$ lemon can be substituted for the sour cream.

Gazpacho

The classic cold soup of Spain, only for those who enjoy the taste of garlic.

50 g (2 oz.) fresh white breadcrumbs
2 tablespoons white wine vinegar
3 chopped cloves garlic
1 large cucumber
1 green pepper
1 Spanish onion
125 ml ($\frac{1}{4}$ pint) olive oil
800 g (2 lbs.) ripe tomatoes
Iced water
Salt and pepper

Soften the breadcrumbs in the vinegar. Combine in a pestle and mortar the breadcrumbs, garlic, $\frac{1}{2}$ cucumber chopped, $\frac{1}{2}$ green pepper chopped, the onion chopped. Pound to a smooth paste and then rub through a fine sieve. Add the olive oil drop by drop stirring continually. Peel and seed the tomatoes and rub through a sieve and add to the paste, thin to the consistency of thin cream with iced water.

Season with salt and pepper and mix in the remaining cucumber cut into small dice and the chopped green pepper.

Serve ice cold with an ice cube in each serving and bowl of crisply fried bread croûtons handed separately.

Note: This soup can be made in a liquidizer/food processor.

Combine the breadcrumbs, wine vinegar, garlic, half the chopped cucumber, half the chopped green pepper and the chopped onion in the liquidizer. Blend at medium speed for 3 minutes. Add the olive oil in teaspoons blending between each addition.

Peel and seed the tomatoes. Add to the other ingredients and blend for a further 2 minutes at medium speed.

Season, thin if necessary with iced water and add the remaining chopped cucumber and green pepper.

Mock Gazpacho

2 tins consommé, or 750 ml (1$\frac{1}{2}$ pints) consommé
3 tomatoes
$\frac{1}{4}$ cucumber
1 tablespoon chopped green pepper
1 tablespoon chopped pimento
2 cloves garlic
Salt and freshly ground black pepper
1 tablespoon sherry (optional)

Skin the tomatoes and remove all the seeds. Cut the flesh into very small dice. Peel and grate the cucumber. Put the garlic through a garlic press, or chop it very very finely. Combine all the ingredients in a bowl and season with salt and pepper.

Chill the soup until set and serve chilled in soup cups.

Iced Haddock Soup

100 g ($\frac{1}{4}$ lb.) smoked haddock
500 ml (1 pint) milk
250 ml ($\frac{1}{2}$ pint) yoghurt
1 cucumber pickled in dill vinegar
2 tablespoons finely chopped parsley
1 tablespoon chives
$\frac{1}{2}$ tablespoon grated onion
Black pepper
Lemon juice
Red caviar for garnish

Poach the haddock in the milk. Cool, strain off and reserve the milk and flake the haddock into small pieces. Add the yoghurt to the milk and mix well. Add the haddock, chopped cucumber, parsley, chives and onion.

Season quite heavily with freshly ground black pepper and a little lemon juice. Serve well chilled with a garnish of red caviar.

Iced Yoghurt and Prawn Soup

500 ml (1 pint) yoghurt
250 ml ($\frac{1}{2}$ pint) single cream
100 g ($\frac{1}{4}$ lb.) prawns
1 medium cucumber
1 tablespoon chopped chives
Salt and pepper

Combine the yoghurt and cream. Mix well. Peel and grate the cucumber. Mix it into the yoghurt with the prawns and chives. Season with salt and pepper.

Serve well chilled with a garnish of chopped mint or with a little paprika sprinkled over each serving.

Vichyssoise

4 leeks
1 large onion
25 g (1 oz.) butter
3 potatoes
750 ml (1½ pints) chicken stock
250 ml (½ pint) cream
Salt and pepper
2 tablespoons chopped chives

Discard the green leaves of the leeks, and put the remainder through a mincer with the onion. Melt the butter in a heavy saucepan. Add the minced leeks and onions and cook over a low flame until soft.

Peel, slice and chop the potatoes. Add them to the leeks and onions and pour over the stock. Cover and simmer for 30 minutes.

Purée the vegetables through a fine sieve or food mill, or in an electric liquidizer. Add the cream, season with salt and pepper and chill well. Just before serving mix in the chopped chives.

Fruit Soup

Fruit soups are widely served in Scandinavian countries. They make a light rather tart beginning to a summer meal and their colour is attractive. They can be served hot or cold.

Plums, damsons, red currants or crab-apples can be used as a basis for the soup but my favourite is one made with sour morello cherries.

400 g (1 lb.) cooking cherries or 2 tins morello cherries
1·5 litres (3 pints) water – or water and juice from the fruit
1 cinnamon stick
Grated rind of 1 lemon
100 g (¼ lb.) sugar
15 g (½ oz.) arrowroot
125 ml (¼ pint) white or red wine

Wash and stone the cherries. Combine the fruit, water, cinnamon, lemon rind and sugar in a heavy saucepan. Bring to the boil and simmer slowly for 20 minutes. Remove the cinnamon.

Rub the fruit through a fine hair sieve. Mix the arrowroot with a little water to form a smooth paste. Add to the sieved purée and cook over a low flame for 5 minutes, stirring continually until the soup is thickened and smooth.

Add the wine. Reheat but do not boil.

CHAPTER FOUR

HORS D'OEUVRES

The word literally translated from the French (according to my dictionary) means an 'outside' dish. Too often it is used to cover the whole field of first courses and starter dishes. I feel that 'hors d'oeuvres' should only be used when describing a first course consisting of a number of small dishes from which everyone makes a selection according to their own particular taste. A more delightful and romantic name, though sadly not in common use, is 'Spurs of Bacchus' so named because many of the dishes encourage a thirst by their rather salty nature.

This way of serving a combination of different dishes has for years been rather the prerogative of hotels and restaurants but now it is appearing with more regularity in private houses. All the dishes can be prepared in advance, most are inexpensive and although they take time and patience to prepare are well within the capabilities of the plainest of cooks. There is also the advantage of being able to cater for everyone's tastes.

Presentation is of paramount importance. A well arranged and prettily served hors d'oeuvre is delightful to see and tickling to the most jaded of palates. One that is badly displayed and muckily arranged can ruin a whole meal.

The number of dishes served depends very much on the occasion. For a simple family meal I provide as few as four. For a buffet supper party or grand dinner, I have as many as twenty choices. As always, with a first course, it is important to bear in mind what is to follow and not to have any basic ingredient in the hors d'oeuvre which appears as part of the main course. For instance keep clear of salads, lettuce, tomatoes, cucumber, etc. if you are serving a salad as a vegetable accompaniment to the main course.

Try to vary your hors d'oeuvre selection as much as possible and as a backbone serve one dish of a meat hors d'oeuvre, one of fish, one of mixed vegetables and one of raw salad stuff, eggs or vegetables. Avoid serving more than one dish with the same sauce.

I have included a list of suggested combinations of hors d'oeuvre dishes for use as a basic guide. Almost certainly, you will soon find your own favourite combination. Probably you could also adapt many of your own recipes, and those in different sections of this book, and include them in your selection.

As a rule the quantities in these recipes are such that four dishes will make an ample hors d'oeuvre for four people. Should you wish to serve one of the dishes as a first course by itself, doubling the quantities should allow enough for four helpings.

PRESENTATION OF HORS D'OEUVRES

You can buy special sectional dishes, mostly imported from Italy and Scandinavia, for serving hors d'oeuvres. They are made in china, glass and plastic. Any small dishes or bowls can be used and the more varied they are the better. Hors d'oeuvres should be gay to look at. I have a number of antique oval plates which were used as stands for sauce boats and I find these very useful. It is important that the plates or dishes should not be too large for what they hold.

Arrangement and garnish are also, as I have said, of the utmost importance. A tin of sardines dumped on a plate does nothing to encourage the gastric juices. The same sardines arranged in a cartwheel pattern, interspersed with thin rolls of smoked meat or smoked salmon and decorated with chopped hard boiled eggs, tomatoes sliced or quartered, capers, sliced stuffed olives, wedges of lemon, etc., will make you feel deliciously hungry. Even the simplest dish rewards attention paid to its decoration, and because the hors d'oeuvre is made up of *small* dishes, trouble must be taken to chop finely, to cut thinly and to keep dice really small. All the trouble you take will be worth while when you finally lay out the dishes before the meal.

If possible serve hors d'oeuvres from a side table. Keep the dishes covered and chilled until it is time to serve them, then arrange them in an attractive formation and let everyone help themselves.

Accompany hors d'oeuvres with a variety of breads and plenty of butter.

BREADS TO SERVE WITH HORS D'OEUVRES

French bread
Crisp rolls
Thin slices of brown and white rye bread
Hot toast
Pumpernickel
Danish rye bread
All crisp bread

READY MADE HORS D'OEUVRES

Many delicatessen shops have a large selection of meat and vegetable salads, ready made, which are perfect for an hors d'oeuvre. Allow 200 g (8 oz.) of each one for 4 people.

Delicatessen shops also sell loose olives, marinated herring fillets, pâtés and smoked meats and sausages of all kinds. Many have their own home made brands of fish and meat pastes. Ask for the paper and skin of sausages to be removed whenever possible before slicing. Have all meats cut thinly.

SELECTIONS OF HORS D'OEUVRE DISHES

1. Stuffed eggs
   Sardines in aspic
   Smoked ham
   Tomato salad

2. Cabbage salad with whipped cream dressing
   Mushroom and pepper salad
   Slices of pâté

Salt herrings with sweet pickles
Frankfurter and potato salad

3. Tomato salad
   Radishes and olives au naturel
   Salmon mayonnaise
   Mixed meat salad with sour cream
   Anchovy and eggs

4. Whipped cream cheese and olives
   Sardines
   Cauliflower in vinaigrette sauce
   Meat balls with mayonnaise and beetroot
   Frankfurter salad

5. Pickled dill cucumber with pâté
   Anchovy à la russe
   Cold meat in sauce Chantilly
   Spring salad
   Rolled mortadella

6. Pickled red cabbage
   Celery in cheese dressing
   Stuffed eggs
   Beef in vinaigrette sauce

7. Prawns or shellfish with mayonnaise
   Anchovy in cucumber cases
   Mushroom and bean salad
   Meat balls with sour cream and horseradish
   Tuna fish
   Red pepper and sweetcorn salad

8. Artichoke hearts à la tartare
   A tin of marinated herring fillets
   Beetroot and hard boiled eggs
   Slices of cheese

Anchovy and Eggs

1 tin anchovies
3 hard boiled eggs
2 tablespoons olive oil
2 teaspoons vinegar
Freshly ground black pepper
1 tablespoon chopped parsley

Drain the anchovies and cut them into small pieces. Chop the hard boiled eggs. Arrange the anchovies and eggs in a serving dish, taking care not to mess up the eggs.

Combine the olive oil and vinegar. Season with pepper. Mix well and pour over the anchovies and eggs. Sprinkle with chopped parsley and serve chilled.

Anchovies with Apples

This is a good combination, the sweetness of the apples takes away the saltiness of the anchovies.

2 crisp eating apples
1 tin anchovies
125 ml ($\frac{1}{4}$ pint) mayonnaise

Peel and core the apples. Cut them into small dice. Drain the anchovies and cut them into small pieces. Fold the apples and anchovies into the mayonnaise. Arrange in a serving dish and chill before serving.

Anchovies à La Russe

Another anchovy/apple combination.

1 tin anchovy fillets
1 crisp eating apple
4 cooked new potatoes
125 ml ($\frac{1}{4}$ pint) mayonnaise
1 tablespoon fresh or sour cream
2 tablespoons chopped chives or spring onion tops

Peel and core the apple, and cut it into small dice. Cut the potatoes into small dice. Combine the mayonnaise with the cream and season if necessary. Fold in the apple and potatoes and arrange in a serving dish.

Drain the anchovy fillets. Cut them into thin strips and arrange them over the apples and potatoes. Sprinkle with the chives and serve chilled.

Artichoke Hearts à La Tartare

1 small tin artichoke hearts
125 ml ($\frac{1}{4}$ pint) mayonnaise
1 tablespoon chopped mixed capers and gherkins
Chopped parsley

Drain the artichokes and cut them into small dice. Add the chopped capers and gherkins to the mayonnaise. Mix well and add the artichokes. Serve in a shallow dish with parsley sprinkled over the surface. Chill well.

Asparagus Vinaigrette

1 tin asparagus spears
3 tablespoons olive oil
1 tablespoon white wine vinegar
1 teaspoon Dijon mustard
Salt and freshly ground black pepper

Drain the asparagus and arrange it in a shallow dish. Blend in the olive oil with the mustard. Add the vinegar and season with salt and pepper. Pour over the asparagus and chill before serving.

Beef in Vinaigrette Sauce

4 thin slices of tender beef (corned beef or boiled brisket may be used instead)
3 tablespoons olive oil
1 tablespoon white wine vinegar

1 teaspoon Dijon mustard
Salt and freshly ground black pepper
2 tablespoons chopped parsley, capers and gherkins

Cut the beef into thin matchstick strips and arrange in a shallow dish. Add the olive oil to the mustard, mix in the vinegar and season with salt and freshly ground black pepper. Add the chopped parsley, capers and gherkins, mix well and pour over the beef. Chill well before serving.

Beef in Creamed Horseradish Sauce

4 thin slices tender beef (corned beef or boiled brisket may be used instead)
125 ml ($\frac{1}{4}$ pint) double cream
2 tablespoons horseradish sauce
Salt and pepper
Parsley

Cut the beef into thin matchstick strips. Whip the cream, mix in the horseradish sauce and season with salt and pepper. Add the beef and serve chilled with a garnish of chopped parsley.

Beetroot

Beetroot can be bought raw or ready cooked from green-grocers. It can also be bought in jars or tins but take care that it is not pickled in vinegar. Raw beetroot should be baked with its skin on in a slow oven until it is tender. When cold the skin will easily rub off. Because of its rather sweet taste it needs to be quite highly seasoned. Pickled beetroot can be cut into thin matchstick strips and served by itself with a garnish of chopped parsley.

Beetroot, Apple and Celery Salad

1 medium beetroot (cooked)
1 crisp eating apple
2 sticks celery

A few chopped walnuts
3 tablespoons olive oil
1 tablespoon lemon juice or white vinegar
Salt and freshly ground black pepper

Cut the beetroot into small dice. Peel, core and dice the apple, and chop the celery. Combine the olive oil and lemon juice or vinegar and season with salt and pepper. Mix all the ingredients together, and chill before serving.

Beetroot and Hard Boiled Eggs

1 medium beetroot (cooked)
2 hard boiled eggs
125 ml ($\frac{1}{4}$ pint) mayonnaise
2 tablespoons cream
Salt and freshly ground black pepper
1 tablespoon chopped parsley

Cut the beetroot into small dice. Chop the hard boiled eggs. Add the cream to the mayonnaise, season highly with salt and freshly ground black pepper. Fold the beetroot and eggs into the mayonnaise, and arrange in a serving dish.
Sprinkle with chopped parsley and serve cold.

Baby Beetroot with Sour Cream

Choose really tiny beetroot, ones the size of large marbles are perfect. Larger beetroot will need to be cut into balls or chopped.

12 baby beetroot
250 ml ($\frac{1}{2}$ pint) sour cream
1 tablespoon lemon juice
3 tablespoons chopped spring onions
Salt and pepper

Wash the beetroot and trim the stalks leaving at least 2·5 cm (1 inch) of stalk attached to the root. Cook the beetroot in boiling water for 1 hour. Cool and rub off the skins.

Combine the sour cream, lemon juice and spring onions.
Season well with salt and pepper.
Pour the sauce over the beetroot and serve chilled.

Broad Bean Salad

200 g ($\frac{1}{2}$ lb.) cooked broad beans
3 tablespoons olive oil
1 tablespoon white wine vinegar
Salt and freshly ground black pepper
1 tablespoon chopped chives

Remove the skins from the broad beans. Combine the olive
oil and vinegar. Season with salt and pepper and mix well.
Pour the dressing over the broad beans. Sprinkle with the
chopped chives.
Chill well before serving.

Broad Beans with Bacon

200 g ($\frac{1}{2}$ lb.) cooked skinned broad beans
2 rashers bacon
3 tablespoons olive oil
1 tablespoon wine vinegar
1 teaspoon French mustard
1 teaspoon chervil
Salt and freshly ground black pepper

Fry the bacon in its own fat until it is crisp. Leave to cool.
Remove the rind and chop into small pieces. Combine the
olive oil, vinegar, French mustard and chervil. Season with
salt and freshly ground black pepper.
Add the beans and bacon to the dressing and mix well.
Arrange in a serving dish and chill before serving.

Cabbage Salad with Whipped Cream Dressing

$\frac{1}{4}$ firm white cabbage
2 eating apples
125 ml ($\frac{1}{4}$ pint) cream
Juice of 1 orange and $\frac{1}{2}$ lemon

Shred the cabbage finely. Peel, core and dice the apples. Whip the cream and mix it with the orange and lemon juice. Fold the cabbage and apples into the whipped cream and pile the salad onto a serving plate.

Carrots

Cooked carrots can be used, cut into very small dice, in most combination vegetable dishes to be served in a mayonnaise or cream dressing. Raw carrot, scraped and cut into very thin julienne strips can be served by itself.

Cauliflower in Vinaigrette Sauce

½ cauliflower
Salted water
3 tablespoons olive oil
1 tablespoon vinegar
Salt and pepper
1 tablespoon chopped pimento

Break the cauliflower into florets. Cook them in boiling salted water until *just* tender (the cauliflower should still be crisp) and drain well.

Combine the olive oil and vinegar and season with salt and pepper. Toss the cauliflower in the dressing whilst it is still warm. Arrange in a dish and sprinkle over the chopped pimento. Chill well before serving.

Celeriac in Mustard Sauce

½ celeriac root
Salted water
125 ml (¼ pint) mayonnaise
1 tablespoon Dijon mustard

Cut the celeriac into thin matchstick strips. Boil until just tender in salted water, about five minutes. Drain and cool.

Mix the mustard with the mayonnaise and add the celeriac. Chill well before serving.

Celery Salad

4 crisp sticks celery
1 hard boiled egg
125 ml ($\frac{1}{4}$ pint) mayonnaise
2 tablespoons double cream
Salt and pepper
Finely chopped parsley

Wash and chop the celery small. Chop the hard boiled egg.
Add the cream to the mayonnaise, season with salt and pepper
and mix in the celery and egg. Arrange in a shallow dish and
sprinkle with chopped parsley.
Chill before serving.

Celery in Cheese Dressing

4 sticks celery
3 tablespoons olive oil
1 tablespoon vinegar
Salt and pepper
2 tablespoons mashed blue cheese

Wash and cut the celery into thin slices. Combine the olive
oil, vinegar and blue cheese, mix well and season with salt and
pepper. Pour the dressing over the celery and leave it to steep
for at least half an hour.

Cheeses

Thin slices of close grained cheeses make a good dish for an
hors d'oeuvre selection. Choose Emmenthal, Gruyère,
caraway seed, or Austrian smoked cheese.
Arrange the slices in a dish. Garnish with radishes or spring
onions.

Chipolata and Cabbage Salad

6 cooked chipolata sausages
100g (4 oz.) or 6 tablespoons shredded white cabbage
1 tablespoon chopped tinned pimento
1 tablespoon chopped onion
3 tablespoons olive oil
1 tablespoon vinegar
1 teaspoon mustard
Salt and pepper

Cut the sausages into thin slices. Combine and mix the olive oil, vinegar, and mustard and season with salt and pepper. Pour the dressing over all the ingredients and mix well. Arrange in a serving dish.

Cold Meats, Poultry, or Fish in Sauce Chantilly

This recipe is useful for using up odd left-overs.

150–200 g (6–8 oz.) cold cooked meat, poultry, or fish
125 ml ($\frac{1}{4}$ pint) mayonnaise
1$\frac{1}{2}$ tablespoons grated fresh horseradish, or horseradish sauce
3 tablespoons double cream
Salt and pepper

Cut the meat or poultry into very small dice or flake the fish. Combine the mayonnaise with the horseradish. Whip the cream and fold it into the mayonnaise. Season with salt and pepper. Fold the meat into the mayonnaise. Arrange in a serving dish and serve chilled.

Note: Chopped spring onions, cooked vegetables, sweet-corn etc. can be added with the meat or fish.

Cooked Vegetable Salad (*Macédoine*)

2 boiled carrots
100 g (4 oz.) cooked French beans
100 g (4 oz.) cooked peas

1 apple
2 tablespoons pickled cucumber
125 ml ($\frac{1}{4}$ pint) mayonnaise
125 ml ($\frac{1}{4}$ pint) double cream
Salt and pepper

Cut the carrots into small dice, and chop the beans. Peel and core the apple and cut into small dice. Chop the cucumber. Whip the cream and combine it with the mayonnaise. Mix well and season with salt and pepper.

Fold the carrots, beans, peas, apple and cucumber into the mayonnaise and arrange on a serving dish.

Cucumber in Sour Cream

1 cucumber
3 tablespoons sour cream
Salt and white pepper
1 teaspoon white wine vinegar
Chopped dill or parsley

Peel the cucumber and cut into paper-thin slices. Arrange in a shallow serving dish. Combine the sour cream and vinegar and season with salt and pepper. Pour the sour cream over the cucumber and sprinkle with chopped dill or parsley. Serve at once.

Note: If the cucumber is left standing with the cream on it, the dressing will become watery.

Pickled Dill Cucumber in Sour Cream

2 large pickled dill cucumbers
3 tablespoons sour cream
Salt and pepper
Chopped parsley

Drain the cucumbers and cut into dice. Season the sour cream with salt and pepper and mix with the cucumber. Arrange in a shallow serving dish, and sprinkle with chopped parsley. Serve chilled.

Egg Salad

3 hard boiled eggs
3 tablespoons olive oil
1 tablespoon vinegar
Salt and freshly ground black pepper
2 tablespoons chopped parsley

Slice the hard boiled eggs. Combine the olive oil and vinegar. Season with salt and pepper, and mix in the chopped parsley. Pour the dressing over the eggs and chill well before serving.

Fennel Salad

1 fennel root
3 tablespoons olive oil
1 tablespoon vinegar
Salt and pepper
2 tablespoons mashed blue cheese

Remove the outside of the fennel root and trim off the hard base and any green shoots at the top. Cut into thin slices and arrange in a serving dish.

Combine the olive oil, vinegar and blue cheese. Mix well and season with salt and pepper. Pour the dressing over the fennel and serve chilled.

Frankfurter and Potato Salad

8 boiled new potatoes
2 large or 4 small boiled frankfurter sausages
3 tablespoons olive oil
1 tablespoon vinegar
1 teaspoon French mustard
1 teaspoon grated onion
Salt and pepper
2 tablespoons chopped chives
Slice the potatoes and the frankfurters.

Combine the olive oil, vinegar, mustard and grated onion. Season with salt and pepper and pour over the potatoes and frankfurters. Mix well and sprinkle the chives over the top. Chill before serving.

Tinned Marinaded Herring Fillets

Many forms of herring fillets are now being imported from Scandinavia. Varieties include herrings in tomato sauce, with dill, with dill pickles and herring tit bits.

Serve tinned herrings in their own sauce or liquid. Chill before serving and garnish with sprigs of fresh dill or parsley.

Salt Herring with Vinaigrette Dressing

2 salt herring fillets
3 tablespoons olive oil
1 tablespoon vinegar
Freshly ground black pepper
1 tablespoon mixed chopped onion and capers

Press the herring fillets gently to remove excess brine. Cut them across in thin strips. Combine the olive oil, vinegar, chopped onion and capers. Mix well and season with freshly ground black pepper. Pour the dressing over the herring fillets and arrange in a shallow serving dish. Chill well before serving.

Note: A tablespoon of sour cream can be added to the vinaigrette dressing.

Salt Herring Fillets with Apples and Sour Cream

(*See under 'Fish Dishes' page 99*)

Leek Salad

12 very small leeks
3 tablespoons olive oil
1 tablespoon white wine vinegar
Salt and freshly ground black pepper

Clean the leeks well and trim the green ends. Cook in boiling salted water until tender (about 20 minutes) drain well and leave to cool.

Combine the olive oil and vinegar and season with salt and pepper. Pour the dressing over the leeks and chill before serving.

Mixed Meat Salad with Sour Cream

50 g (2 oz.) tongue
50 g (2 oz.) ham
50 g (2 oz.) cooked roast beef or salt beef
125 ml ($\frac{1}{4}$ pint) sour cream; or 125 ml ($\frac{1}{4}$ pint) fresh cream
   soured with lemon juice
Salt, white pepper and paprika
1 tablespoon chopped gherkins (optional)
Lettuce leaves

Cut the meat into thin matchstick strips about 2·5 cm (1 inch) long. Whip the cream and season with salt, white pepper and paprika. Mix the meat with the whipped cream and the chopped gherkins. Arrange on lettuce leaves in a shallow serving dish.

Mushroom and Bean Salad

100 g (4 oz.) fresh button mushrooms
150 g (6 oz.) cooked French beans
1 clove garlic
3 tablespoons olive oil
1 tablespoon vinegar
Salt and pepper
$\frac{1}{2}$ teaspoon chopped tarragon

Wash and slice the mushrooms through the stalks and caps. Cut the beans into 1 cm ($\frac{1}{2}$ inch) pieces. Crush the garlic and mix it well with the oil and vinegar. Add the tarragon and season with salt and pepper. Pour the dressing over the mushrooms and beans and leave to steep for at least half an hour.

Mushroom and Pepper Salad

1 small red pepper
1 large green pepper
100 g (4 oz.) fresh button mushrooms
50 g (2 oz.) cold crisply fried bacon
3 tablespoons olive oil
1 tablespoon vinegar
Salt and pepper

Seed and core the peppers, chop them finely. Wash the mushrooms and cut them into thin slices through the caps and
stalks. Remove the rinds from the bacon and chop it into
small pieces. Combine the oil and vinegar and mix well. Season with salt and pepper.

Arrange the peppers and mushrooms in a serving dish.
Pour over the dressing and sprinkle with the chopped bacon.

Olives

Both green and black olives can be served, au naturel, as an
hors d'oeuvre. Choose large firm ones, and if possible buy
them loose from a delicatessen shop, as they taste better than
the bottled ones.

Arrange them (chilled) in a serving dish, allowing about
3 for each serving.

Pâtés or Terrines

Cut thin slices of pâté or terrine, and arrange them on a serving dish and garnish with sprigs of fresh parsley. Allow one
slice per helping.

Pickled Dill Cucumber with Pâté

3 large pickled cucumbers
1 small tin pâté

Cut the cucumbers into 1 cm ($\frac{1}{2}$ inch) slices or 2·5 cm (1 inch) squares, depending on their shape. Cover each slice with a layer of pâté and arrange on a shallow serving dish.

Pickled Red Cabbage

1 small red cabbage
250 ml ($\frac{1}{2}$ pint) cider vinegar
2 tablespoons olive oil
Salt and freshly ground black pepper

Trim and wash the cabbage, removing any coarse leaves and all the core. Shred very finely and put into a bowl.

Bring the vinegar to the boil. Pour over the cabbage and leave it to steep for 4–5 hours, then drain well. Add the olive oil to the cabbage. Season with salt and pepper and mix well. Chill before serving.

Prawns or Dublin Bay Prawns Au Naturel

Serve cooked prawns or Dublin Bay prawns in their shells. Allow 4 prawns or 1 Dublin Bay prawn per serving. Arrange in a circular serving dish with a small dish of mayonnaise in the centre.

Prawns and Mushrooms

200 g ($\frac{1}{2}$ lb.) small button mushrooms
1 small clove garlic
4 tablespoons olive oil
2 tablespoons lemon juice
Salt and freshly ground black pepper
150 g (6 oz.) peeled prawns
Chopped parsley

Wash and dry the mushrooms. Cut into thin slices through the caps and stalks. Squeeze the garlic in a garlic press and mix with the olive oil and lemon juice. Season with salt and pepper. Pour the dressing over the mushrooms and leave to marinade for at least 1 hour in a cool place. Mix in the peeled prawns and sprinkle over the chopped parsley. Serve chilled.

Radishes Au Naturel

I have yet to come across a nicer way of serving radishes than on a bed of crushed ice with plenty of salted butter at hand. Take a radish by its stalk and make a neat incision half way through the root. Insert a thin slice of butter and pop the whole thing into your mouth – the taste is fantastic.

Radishes come in many shapes and sizes. Beware of those that are too large as they are often hollow inside. Perfect radishes are a deep rosy red and no more than 2 cm (three quarters of an inch) long.

1–2 bunches radishes (about 24)

Wash the radishes in cold running water. Remove the thin root and trim the stalk to about 1 cm ($\frac{1}{2}$ inch). Serve in a bowl on a bed of crushed ice with salted butter.

Radishes with Sour Cream

2 bunches (24) radishes
1 chopped hard boiled egg
3 tablespoons sour cream
Salt and white pepper
Chopped parsley or chives

Wash the radishes, remove the tops and tails, cut into thin slivers. Mix the radishes with the chopped egg and the sour cream. Season with salt and pepper and chill before serving. Arrange in a shallow serving dish. Garnish with chopped parsley or chives.

Red Pepper and Sweetcorn Salad

1 large sweet red pepper
1 small tin sweetcorn
3 tablespoons olive oil
1 tablespoon vinegar
Salt and pepper

Seed, core and chop the pepper. Drain the sweetcorn and mix it with the pepper.

Combine the olive oil and vinegar and mix well. Season with salt and pepper. Pour the dressing over the pepper and corn and chill well before serving.

Rollmops

Rollmops are raw marinated herrings. They can be bought singly in many delicatessen shops, or in jars from most good fishmongers. Arrange rollmops in a shallow serving dish. Garnish with a little potato salad.

Rolled Bologna Sausage or Mortadella

Bologna sausage is a large mild-tasting, finely-grained, smoked pork sausage with pistachio nuts. It is stocked by most good delicatessen shops.

100 g ($\frac{1}{4}$ lb.) thinly cut Bologna sausage or mortadella
100 g ($\frac{1}{4}$ lb.) cream cheese
8 green olives stuffed with pimento
Salt and pepper

Remove the skin from the sausage (cut the mortadella into 5 cm (2 inch) circles with a pastry cutter – use the trimmings for mortadella salad). Chop the stuffed olives and mix them with the cream cheese. Season with salt and pepper.

Spread some of the cream cheese on the sausage slices and roll them up neatly. Arrange the rolls on a shallow serving dish.

Salami, Garlic or Smoked Sausages

Arrange wafer thin slices of sausage on a serving plate. Garnish with sprigs of fresh parsley.

Salmon Mayonnaise

150 g (6 oz.) cold salmon or 1 tin salmon
2 cold boiled potatoes
125 ml ($\frac{1}{4}$ pint) mayonnaise
2 tablespoons chopped chives

Cut the salmon into small pieces and the potatoes into small dice. Mix both with the mayonnaise. Arrange in a serving dish and sprinkle with the chives. Chill before serving.

SARDINES

Tinned sardines can be served straight from the tin just as they are. Drain off most of the oil, and arrange them attractively in a serving dish. Garnish with chopped parsley or capers.

The cold sardine dishes under the fish section (pages 103–4) can be used for hors d'oeuvres (but halve the quantities).

Sardines in Aspic Jelly

8 sardines
50 g (2 oz.) thinly sliced tongue
250 ml ($\frac{1}{2}$ pint) aspic jelly
2 tomatoes
8 thin slices cucumber

Drain the sardines and roll each one carefully in a slice of tongue. Pour a shallow layer of aspic jelly into an oblong tin or dish and leave to set. Arrange the sardines on the jelly. Cover with the rest of the aspic and leave to set.

Cut out the sardines surrounded by the aspic. Arrange them on a serving dish. Garnish with thin slices of tomato and cucumber.

Saveloys

Saveloys are highly spiced boiling sausages sold at all delicatessen shops.

Cook them in boiling water until they are tender. (How long depends on the size.) Leave them to cool then cut into thin slices.

Shellfish

Cut cooked shelled lobster, prawns, scampi, etc. into small dice. Combine the shellfish with 250 ml ($\frac{1}{2}$ pint) mayonnaise, season well, and serve chilled.

Note: All shellfish can also be served shelled either plain or in a French dressing. See section on Shellfish (page 123) for directions for preparation.

Potted Shrimps

100 g (4 oz.) pot of potted shrimps
1 lemon
Fresh parsley

Break up the potted shrimps with a fork and arrange them in a dish. Garnish with quarters of lemon and fresh sprigs of parsley.

Small Swedish Meat Balls

These small balls are finicky to make but can be prepared well in advance and can be served in a variety of sauces. They make a useful addition to an hors d'oeuvre selection. Ask your butcher to mince the meat.

25 g (1 oz.) butter
1 large finely chopped onion
4 tablespoons fresh white breadcrumbs
125 ml ($\frac{1}{4}$ pint) single cream
200 g ($\frac{1}{2}$ lb.) finely minced lean beef

100 g ($\frac{1}{4}$ lb.) finely minced pork
100 g ($\frac{1}{4}$ lb.) finely minced veal
1 beaten egg
1 tablespoon finely chopped parsley
Salt and pepper
A pinch of nutmeg
Flour
40 g (1$\frac{1}{2}$ oz.) butter for frying

Melt the butter in a saucepan. Add the chopped onion and fry gently over a low heat until soft and transparent – about 10 minutes. Soak the breadcrumbs in the cream and mix gently with a fork until they are soft. Combine the onions, soaked breadcrumbs, meat, egg and parsley in a large bowl. Season with salt, pepper and nutmeg and mix well.

Form the meat into small balls about 1 cm ($\frac{1}{2}$ inch) in diameter and roll them in flour. Melt 40 g (1$\frac{1}{2}$ oz.) butter in a large frying pan. Add the meat balls and fry over a high flame until they are brown, adding a little more butter if necessary. Shake the pan frequently to ensure that the balls are cooked all over and keep their shape. Drain the balls on kitchen paper and leave them to cool.

Meat Balls with Cucumber and Sour Cream
Recipe for small meat balls (quantities halved)
125 ml ($\frac{1}{4}$ pint) sour cream
4 tablespoons peeled and diced fresh cucumber, or dill pickled cucumbers
Salt and pepper

Mix the sour cream with the diced cucumber, season with salt and pepper and pour over the meat balls. Arrange in a serving dish.

Meat Balls with Mayonnaise and Beetroot
Recipe for small meat balls (quantities halved)
125 ml ($\frac{1}{4}$ pint) mayonnaise
3 tablespoons diced cooked beetroot
Salt and pepper

Gently mix the mayonnaise with the meat balls and diced beetroot, season with salt and pepper and arrange in a serving dish.

Meat Balls with Sour Cream and Horseradish
  Recipe for small meat balls (quantities halved)
  1 tablespoon horseradish sauce
  125 ml ($\frac{1}{4}$ pint) sour cream
  Salt and pepper
  Chopped parsley

Combine the horseradish with the sour cream, season with salt and pepper and mix well. Pour the cream over the meat balls and turn them gently so that they are well coated. Arrange in a serving dish and sprinkle with chopped parsley.

Smoked Ham

  100 g (4 oz.) raw smoked ham – Parma, Westphalian, etc.
  Fresh parsley

Cut the ham into very thin slices. Arrange the slices either flat, rolled or in the shape of coronets on a serving dish. Garnish with sprigs of fresh parsley.

Smoked Sprats

Smoked sprats can be bought fresh or tinned from good delicatessen shops. Drain off the oil if the sprats are tinned. Serve them as they are, with a garnish of lemon wedges and a horseradish sauce (see page 219).

Spring Salad

  $\frac{1}{2}$ cauliflower
  3 spring onions
  $\frac{1}{4}$ green pepper
  $\frac{1}{4}$ red pepper
  2 tomatoes

3 tablespoons olive oil
1 tablespoon vinegar
Salt and pepper

Separate the cauliflower into florets and boil in salted water until tender (12–15 minutes), then drain and leave to cool. Trim the spring onions and chop finely. Seed and core the green and red peppers and chop finely. Remove the cores of the tomatoes and chop roughly. Combine the olive oil with the vinegar and mix well. Season with salt and pepper and pour the dressing over the other ingredients. Mix well and arrange in a serving dish. Serve chilled.

Stuffed Eggs

Any of the selection of stuffed hard boiled eggs found under the Egg Section (page 188) can be used to form part of a selection of hors d'oeuvres.

Summer Sausage Salad

6 cooked chipolata sausages
¼ cucumber
1 large stick celery
50 g (2 oz.) Cheddar cheese
50 g (2 oz.) or 3 tablespoons shredded white cabbage
125 ml (¼ pint) mayonnaise
1 tablespoon single cream
Salt and pepper

Cut the chipolatas into chunks, peel and dice the cucumber, dice the cheese and slice the celery. Combine the mayonnaise with the cream, mix well, and season with salt and pepper.

Pour the dressing over the other ingredients, including the cabbage, and mix well. Arrange in a serving dish.

Sweetcorn

Tinned creamed sweetcorn can be served as a dish in a selection of hors d'oeuvres. Add a little double cream to the sweetcorn and season with salt and pepper.

Tinned sweetcorn kernels can be added to mixed vegetable dishes served in a mayonnaise or French dressing.

Bottled baby sweetcorn, available at good grocers and delicatessen shops, can be served as it is.

Tomato Salad

> 3 firm tomatoes
> 3 spring onions or 2 tablespoons chopped onion or chives
> 3 tablespoons olive oil
> 1 tablespoon white wine vinegar
> Salt and freshly ground black pepper

Cut the tomatoes into very thin slices and arrange in a shallow serving dish. Slice the white and green part of the spring onions and sprinkle over the tomatoes. Combine the olive oil and vinegar. Season with salt and pepper and pour over the tomatoes. Serve chilled.

Tomato Slices with Pâté

> 50 g (2 oz.) home-made or bought pâté maison (a coarse grained soft pâté is best)
> 3 large firm tomatoes
> Small sprigs of parsley

Cut off a slice from the head and tail of the tomatoes and discard. Cut the centre into three thick slices.

Spread a small spoonful of pâté on the top of each tomato slice.

Garnish with a small sprig of parsley and arrange on a flat serving dish.

TUNA FISH

Tinned tuna fish is one of the cheapest, most versatile and most delicious of tinned fish. Buy a good quality and drain it well. Serve tuna as it is, garnished with lemon, parsley, and capers, or in a mayonnaise or French dressing.

Tuna with Mayonnaise or French Dressing

1 medium sized tin tuna fish
125 ml ($\frac{1}{4}$ pint) mayonnaise
1 teaspoon lemon juice
Salt and pepper
Lettuce leaves

Drain the tuna and flake roughly with a fork. Combine the fish with the mayonnaise and lemon juice and season with salt and pepper. Arrange on lettuce leaves in a shallow serving dish. Serve cold.

Note: French dressing (3 tablespoons olive oil, 1 tablespoon white wine vinegar, salt and pepper) can be used in the place of the mayonnaise.

Whipped Cream Cheese and Olives

100 g ($\frac{1}{4}$ lb.) cream cheese
125 ml ($\frac{1}{4}$ pint) double cream
Salt, pepper, and paprika
12 pimento- or anchovy-stuffed olives

Whip the cream until stiff and work it into the cheese. Season with salt, pepper and paprika. Chop the olives and mix them with the cheese. Pile onto a serving dish.

OPEN SANDWICHES

In Sweden and the other Scandinavian countries, open sandwiches are frequently served as first courses. An infinite variety of fresh, pickled and smoked meats, fishes, vegetables and salads are used to make the sandwiches, and much of their attraction lies in the garnishing and decoration of the ingredients used.

It is essential to bear these few points in mind if you are planning to include open sandwiches in your menu:

1. The bread you use must be fresh – continental rye brands in both white and brown are the most suitable.

2. The bread *must* have all the crusts removed.

3. The bread must be lavishly spread with *soft* butter – this helps to keep the filling in place.

4. The sandwiches should be served as fresh as possible. If it is necessary to make them in advance, take care not to leave them exposed to the air. Cover them with a light, damp cloth, or wax paper, or seal them in a polythene container.

5. The filling should completely cover the bread and if necessary be kept in place with mayonnaise or some other sauce.

The best way to serve open sandwiches is to make at least four different varieties and either to arrange a selection on individual plates or to pass round a large serving plate with the sandwiches attractively displayed on it.

Open sandwiches make light appetizing snacks for lunches and suppers, but if they are to be served as a course on their own they must be small so as not to deaden the appetite for the rest of the meal.

TO MAKE OPEN SANDWICHES
Chill the bread in the refrigerator before cutting it – this helps to prevent it from crumbling. Use a sharp knife with a serrated edge and cut thin, uniform slices. Butter the bread with plenty of softened butter. Remove the crusts and cut into rounds, triangles or squares. Arrange the filling on the bread and garnish attractively. Open sandwiches, when served as a first course, are usually eaten with a small knife and fork.

SUGGESTIONS FOR FILLINGS
Cold scrambled egg is very useful as a filling for open sandwiches. The easiest way to cut it neatly is to leave the cooked egg to cool in a small buttered oblong cake tin. When cold and set turn out and cut into thin slices.

In addition to the usual garnishes (thinly sliced lemon, olives, gherkins, etc.) the Scandinavians often use chopped and sliced radishes, thinly sliced raw onion rings, thinly sliced rings of baby leeks and green pepper and sprigs of dill.

Caviar mentioned in the recipes is imitation and sold in small glass jars.

The herring fillets can be bought in tins packed in oil and dill.

1. Lettuce leaf topped with hard boiled egg slices, mayonnaise and anchovy fillets.
2. Lettuce leaf topped with smoked salmon, garnished with chopped white of egg and a slice of lemon.
3. Thin slice of salami, folded and garnished with slices of green olives.
4. Lettuce with smoked fillets of eel and slices of cold scrambled egg, garnished with a twist of lemon.
5. Thin slices of Gruyère or Emmenthal cheese garnished with rings of green pepper.
6. Lettuce with prawns and mayonnaise garnished with capers.
7. Thin slices of tomato garnished with chopped raw onion and thin slices of radish.
8. Thin slices of cold potato with red caviar, garnished with thinly cut rings of leeks or spring onions.
9. Thin slices of cold potato with small pieces of herring, garnished with chopped chives and a dab of sour cream.
10. Lettuce topped by caviar and sour cream, garnished with a thin wedge of lemon.
11. Lettuce topped with chopped beetroot and apple in mayonnaise, garnished with a strip of crisply fried cold bacon.
12. Smoked ham garnished with gherkins or pickled cucumber.
13. Chopped lettuce topped with duckling fillet and garnished with chopped raw onions and radishes.
14. Liver pâté garnished with strips of aspic jelly.

15. Thin slices of salt meat garnished with horseradish sauce and chopped chives.
16. Red caviar and sardines garnished with parsley and a thin wedge of lemon.
17. Sardines with mayonnaise and chopped hard boiled egg, garnished with parsley.
18. Thin slices of smoked tongue garnished with redcurrant jelly.
19. Slices of cucumber topped with smoked eel fillet.
20. Chopped cold potato and chopped chives in mayonnaise, garnished with anchovy fillets.
21. Smoked salmon with tinned asparagus, garnished with a thin wedge of lemon.
22. Liver pâté garnished with shredded lettuce and sliced black olives.
23. Shredded lettuce with red caviar and slices of hard boiled egg, and garnished with a dollop of sour cream.
24. Cream cheese topped with sardines and garnished with a thin wedge of lemon and a sprig of parsley.
25. Lettuce topped with small pieces of cold fried fish with a spoonful of sauce tartare, garnished with thin lemon wedges and a few small rings of raw onion.
26. Prawns topped with whipped seasoned cream and garnished with dill or chopped chives.
27. Lettuce topped with red caviar, black caviar and smoked cod's roe, garnished with sour cream and leek rings.
28. A slice of pâté garnished with pickled cucumber and cream cheese.
29. Chopped radishes topped with thin slices of cheese.
30. Crab in mayonnaise garnished with shredded lettuce and sliced green and black olives.
31. Thin rolled slices of salt or cooked beef with pickled cucumber.
32. Cream cheese mixed with chopped green olives and garnished with gherkins.
33. Cold potatoes chopped with dill, in mayonnaise and garnished with prawns.

34. Cold scrambled egg topped with black caviar and garnished with chopped raw onions and a spoonful of sour cream.
35. Alternate slices of garlic sausage and smoked tongue, garnished with gherkins and olives.
36. Thin slices of ham garnished with chopped tinned asparagus and cocktail onions.
37. Lettuce topped with mayonnaise mixed with chopped radishes, chopped green pepper, and chopped meat, and garnished with black olives.
38. Lettuce topped with minced clams and mayonnaise and garnished with thin twists of lemon and chopped chives.
39. Alternate slices of various cheese garnished with thin slices of radishes and gherkins.
40. Smoked salmon with caviar and chopped onions garnished with thin wedges of lemon.

CHAPTER FIVE

FISH

Most fishes make good first course material though to my mind many of the classic sauces are too rich for the beginning of a meal. Take care when buying fish to ensure that it is absolutely fresh. Choose a fishmonger who has a good reputation and a clean shop. Fresh fish have bright eyes and the gleam of salt water on their scales. If you have your fishmonger fillet fish for you, ask for the trimmings, they make very good fish stock and form the basis of many sauces and fish soups.

Clean fish under cold running water. If it has to be kept, unwrap it before putting it in a refrigerator. Frozen fish must be cooked as soon as it has thawed. Fish is cooked when it can be separated easily from the bone; it is difficult to deal with if overcooked and loses a great deal of its flavour.

Allow 100–150 g (4–6 oz. without bones) fish per serving.

THE ART OF FRYING FISH

Fish and chips in a parcel of newspaper are great to eat in the street or on the way home from a day spent in the open air, but they are nothing like fried fish to be eaten as a first course. The secret lies in fast cooking and the use of pure olive oil, never ever lard or dripping and never (except in some specialized dishes) butter.

All fish should be well dried before being floured, dipped in egg and breadcrumbs, or in butter, or merely fried plain. It must be cooked in a really large pan in plenty of oil and, in the case of small fish, in small quantities only. The olive oil should be able to move freely around and over the fish as it cooks.

The oil must be very hot before the fish is put in: when it is hot enough, a thin smoky haze will begin to rise. When the fish is plunged in, the oil's temperature will naturally fall and the heat must therefore be raised to compensate.

KEEPING FRIED FISH HOT. Once the fish is cooked it must be well drained to remove any excess oil. The best way of doing this is to move it straight from the pan onto a plate covered with crumpled absorbent kitchen paper. Small fish which have to be fried in small quantities should be left to drain on the paper in a warm oven until they are ready to serve. If they go limp, three minutes in a really hot oven will help to crispen them up. Oil that has been used for frying can be strained, kept in a cool place, and used again.

POACHING FISH

To prevent fish losing its flavour whilst being poached, and in fact to improve its flavour, poaching is usually done in a court bouillon. Put the fish into warm court bouillon, bring it to the boil and simmer gently until it is just cooked, about 20 minutes per 400 g (1 lb.). Serve poached fish with hollandaise sauce, sauce tartare, mayonnaise, seafood sauce, tomato sauce, egg sauce, prawn sauce. Salmon, sea trout, trout, halibut, turbot and any firm fleshed white fish are suitable.

BAKED FISH

White fish and salmon respond well to baking either in a well-buttered baking dish with a sauce or wrapped in well-buttered aluminium foil. The second method works specially well with turbot and halibut. Bake fish in a moderate oven (180 C., 350 F., Reg. 4) for 15 minutes per 400 g (1 lb.).

STEAMED FISH

Dried fish or fish that is to be served in an exceptionally heavy sauce should be steamed over boiling water in a steamer or a colander with a tight fitting lid. Cook until just tender, about 20 minutes. Steamed fish loses a little of its flavour but it is very easy to digest and has a good firm texture. Add the water over which the fish was steamed to sauces.

Anchovy Salad

1 tin anchovy fillets
2 hard boiled eggs
2 boiled potatoes
1 small onion or 3 spring onions
3 tablespoons olive oil
1 tablespoon vinegar
Pepper

Drain and chop the anchovies, chop the hard boiled eggs, dice the potatoes, and chop the onion. Combine the olive oil with the vinegar. Mix all the ingredients together and season well with pepper (not salt as the anchovies are so salty). Chill before serving.

Janson's Temptation

An old, well-tried Swedish recipe. It is very economical and a good starter in winter.

2 large onions
4 potatoes (old ones)
1 large tin anchovy fillets and the juice
2 tablespoons butter
125 ml ($\frac{1}{4}$ pint) single cream
Pepper
50 g (2 oz.) butter

Peel and thinly slice the onions and potatoes. Butter a casserole dish with the 2 tablespoons butter. Arrange half the potatoes on the bottom. Cover them with the onions and anchovy fillets. Sprinkle with a little pepper and cover with the remaining potatoes. Pour over the juice from the anchovies and half the cream. Dot with the 50 g (2 oz.) butter cut into small pieces. Bake in a medium oven (190 C., 375 F., Reg. 5) for 30 minutes. Pour over the remaining cream. Continue to bake for a further 15 minutes until the potatoes are tender and a golden brown crust has formed on the surface. Serve hot.

CAVIAR

Caviar (need I tell you?) comes from Russia. It is the roe of a noble and very valuable fish, the sturgeon. In this country it is bought in jars or tins and costs a fortune.

Allow 50 g (2 oz.) caviar per person and serve it straight from the jar or in a glass bowl, well surrounded by crushed ice, and wrapped in a white napkin. It must be really well chilled. Accompany caviar with thin freshly made toast, thin wedges of lemon and well-iced vodka.

MOCK CAVIAR OR LUMPFISH ROE. Much smaller grained and more salty than the true caviar, lumpfish roe is a useful substitute for the real thing, as an addition to a selection of hors d'oeuvre dishes and as an ingredient and garnish for many first courses. It is sold in glass jars.

RED CAVIAR. Cheaper than lumpfish roe and useful for hors d'oeuvres and in made up dishes.

Cod à La Grecque

4 small cod steaks
1 onion
½ green pepper
3 ripe tomatoes
2 tablespoons peeled and chopped cucumber
15 g (½ oz.) butter
125 ml (¼ pint) sour cream
½ teaspoon paprika pepper
Salt and pepper

Peel and chop the onion. Seed and core the pepper, and chop finely. Skin and slice the tomatoes. Sprinkle the cucumber with salt and leave to drain in a colander for 20 minutes. Dry well.

Butter a baking dish. Cover the bottom with a layer of chopped onion, pepper and cucumber. Arrange the sliced tomatoes over this layer and place the cod steaks on top.

Sprinkle with salt and pepper. Combine the cream and paprika and pour it over the fish. Cover tightly with a lid or aluminium foil and bake in a moderate oven (180 C., 350 F., Reg. 4) for 25 minutes or until the fish is tender. Serve hot.

Haddock in Sour Cream

150 g (6 oz.) cooked haddock
$\frac{1}{2}$ cucumber
1 tablespoon chopped pimento
1 teaspoon curry paste
1 teaspoon lemon juice
125 ml ($\frac{1}{4}$ pint) sour cream
1 teaspoon chopped chervil
3 chopped spring onions
Salt and pepper
Chopped parsley

Flake the cooked haddock. Peel and dice the cucumber. Arrange the haddock, cucumber and chopped pimento in a serving dish. Dissolve the curry paste in the lemon juice. Add to the sour cream with the chopped chervil and spring onions. Mix well and season with salt and pepper. Pour the sour cream over the fish. Sprinkle the surface with chopped parsley and chill well. Serve with hot crisp rolls.

Baked Turbot or Halibut with Sauce Antonia

800 g–1 kg (1$\frac{1}{2}$–2 lbs.) turbot or halibut on the bone
A sheet of aluminium foil
25 g (1 oz.) butter

SAUCE
Salt and pepper
40 g (1$\frac{1}{2}$ oz.) butter
40 g (1$\frac{1}{2}$ oz.) flour
250 ml ($\frac{1}{2}$ pint) milk
2 tablespoons tomato pickle or chutney

1 tablespoon Dijon mustard
2 tablespoons cream
Parsley
1 lemon

Butter a large sheet of aluminium foil. Place the fish on this and dot with 25 g (1 oz.) butter. Season with salt and pepper. Wrap up neatly and bake the fish in a medium oven (190 C., 375 F., Reg. 5) for 20–30 minutes until the fish is just tender. Remove the black skin carefully.

Melt 40 g (1½ oz.) butter in a saucepan. Add the flour and mix well. Gradually add the milk stirring well over a medium heat until the sauce is thick and smooth. Add the tomato pickle and Dijon mustard. Bring to the boil and cook for 2 minutes. Season with salt and pepper. Add the cream and remove from the heat. Arrange the fish in a serving dish. Spoon over the sauce. Serve hot with a garnish of fresh parsley and lemon wedges.

Note: This sauce can be served with steamed or poached fillets of plaice and sole.

PICKLED HERRINGS

Pickled herrings, filleted and marinaded in a well spiced vinegar, can be bought in jars from most delicatessen stores. They are well flavoured and can be used for many first courses. In composite dishes, care should be taken with seasoning, especially salt.

Pickled Herring Salad

1 jar pickled herrings or 4 pickled herrings
2 hard boiled eggs
3 tomatoes
250 ml (½ pint) sour cream
2 tablespoons tomato ketchup
2 tablespoons made horseradish sauce
1 tablespoon made English mustard
A few drops of Tabasco sauce

Drain the herrings and arrange them in a shallow serving dish. Cut the eggs into thin slices. Peel and slice the tomatoes. Arrange the eggs and tomatoes around the herrings.

Combine the remaining ingredients, mix well and season with a few drops of Tabasco sauce. Pour the dressing over the herrings and serve chilled.

SALT HERRINGS

Pity the poor herring: it is a most neglected fish. It comes in many forms and the salted fillets are most useful for many first course dishes. Most good delicatessen shops sell salted herring fillets and they can be dressed up in the most exotic and palatable ways. Squeeze the fillets gently to remove excess brine and do not use any salt when seasoning sauces that are to accompany the fish.

Salt Herring Fillets with Apples and Sour Cream

4 salt herring fillets
2 crisp eating apples
250 ml ($\frac{1}{2}$ pint) sour cream
Pepper and paprika
$\frac{1}{2}$ teaspoon chopped capers
Chopped dill or parsley

Drain the herring fillets and press gently to remove excess brine. Cut across into thin strips. Peel, core and slice the apples. Arrange the herring strips and slices of apple in a shallow serving dish. Season the sour cream with pepper and paprika. Pour the cream over the herring and apples. Garnish with the chopped capers, and chopped dill or parsley. Serve chilled with thin slices of brown bread and butter.

Note: To serve as one of a selection of hors d'oeuvre dishes, halve the quantities and chop the herring fillets and the apple.

Baked Mackerel with Olives

4 small mackerel
2 dozen pitted green olives
2 dozen pitted black olives
2 tablespoons olive oil
Salt and pepper

Clean and gut the mackerel. Arrange them in an oiled fire-proof serving dish. Stuff 6 green olives into the cavity of each fish. Arrange the black olives around the fish. Sprinkle with salt and pepper and with the olive oil. Bake for 20–30 minutes in a medium oven (190 C., 375 F., Reg. 5) basting frequently with the juices in the pan.
Serve hot.

Cold Baked Mackerel

4 small mackerel
75 g (3 oz.) butter
200 g ($\frac{1}{2}$ lb.) button mushrooms
1 clove garlic
2 tablespoons grated onion
250 ml ($\frac{1}{2}$ pint) sour cream
Salt, pepper and paprika
Parsley

Clean and gut the mackerel leaving the heads and tails on. Soften 50 g (2 oz.) butter and season it with salt and pepper. Rub the fish inside and out with the butter. Wrap the fish in aluminium foil and bake in a moderate oven (180 C., 350 F., Reg. 4) for 20 minutes. Unwrap and leave to cool. Arrange the fish in a shallow serving dish.

Wash and dry the mushrooms. Cut them into thin slices through the caps and stalks. Melt 25 g (1 oz.) butter and cook the mushrooms over a medium heat for 3 minutes. Drain well and leave to cool. Press the garlic through a garlic press or pound in a pestle and mortar. Combine the sour cream, mushrooms, grated onion and garlic. Season with salt, pepper and a

pinch of paprika. Pour the sauce over the mackerel and
garnish with sprigs of parsley. Serve chilled.

Fillets of Mackerel with Cucumber and Sour Cream

4 small mackerel or 2 large ones, or 2 tins drained Portuguese mackerel fillets
50 g (2 oz.) butter
Salt and freshly ground black pepper
A little olive oil
125 ml ($\frac{1}{4}$ pint) sour cream
1 cucumber
1 lemon

Clean the fish leaving on the head and tail. Stuff the cavities
with the butter seasoned with a little salt and pepper. Wrap
the fish in a sheet of aluminium foil brushed with a little olive
oil. Bake in a moderate oven (180 C., 350 F., Reg. 4) for 20
minutes. Leave to cool. Remove the skin, heads and tails and
gently ease the fillets off the bones.
   Peel the cucumber and cut the flesh into small dice. Add to
the sour cream and season with salt and pepper. Arrange the
mackerel fillets in a shallow serving dish. Mash them with the
sour cream and cucumber and garnish with thin slices of
lemon. Serve chilled with thin slices of buttered brown bread.

SALMON AND SEA TROUT
Unfortunately, both these delicious, rich, softly pink fish are
in the luxury price bracket even at the height of the season. Of
the two I prefer the sea trout which has more flavour and is
less rich than the larger salmon. Both are good served hot or
cold, cold being the more economical method.
   The fish must be cooked in a court bouillon and if possible
whole in a fish kettle or on a rack in a large pan. If neither of
those is available it is better to wrap them in oiled aluminium
foil and bake them in an oven than spoil them by cutting them
into portions. Allow 700 g (1$\frac{3}{4}$ lb.) salmon or sea trout for 4
servings. If a whole fish is cooked the remainder may be used

in a variety of ways. When buying salmon or sea trout find out if it has been frozen. Unless great care has been taken with the freezing and defrosting of these fish, the texture and taste is impaired and the cost of the fish should be greatly reduced.

Tinned Salmon and Egg Au Gratin

200 g (8 oz.) tin salmon
3 hard boiled eggs
3 tomatoes
25 g (1 oz.) butter
25 g (1 oz.) flour
200 g ($\frac{1}{2}$ pint) milk
100 g (4 oz.) grated cheese
Salt and pepper
A pinch of nutmeg

Drain the salmon. Chop the hard boiled eggs and tomatoes. Arrange salmon, eggs, and tomatoes in a buttered fireproof serving dish.

Melt the butter in a heavy pan. Add the flour and mix well. Gradually add the milk, stirring continually over a medium heat until the sauce is thick and smooth. Bring to the boil and add 50 g (2 oz.) cheese. Continue to cook until the cheese has melted. Season with salt, pepper and a pinch of nutmeg. Pour the sauce over the fish and sprinkle the remaining cheese over the surface. Brown in a hot oven (230 C., 450 F., Reg. 8) for 10 minutes. Serve hot.

Rich Salmon Mould

400 g (1 lb.) fresh cooked salmon (or half tinned salmon and half tuna)
250 ml ($\frac{1}{2}$ pint) double cream
1 tablespoon tomato ketchup
A few drops of Tabasco sauce
Salt and pepper
$\frac{1}{2}$ pint thick aspic jelly
$\frac{1}{4}$ cucumber
2 tablespoons sour cream

Skin the salmon and remove all the bones. Mash the flesh until almost smooth, with a fork or through a coarse sieve. Whip the cream until stiff. Mix in the salmon. Season with tomato ketchup, Tabasco sauce, salt, and pepper. Chill the aspic jelly until almost set. Fold in the salmon mixture and spoon the mixture into a dampened ring mould. Leave in a cool place until set.

Turn the mould out onto a circular serving dish. Peel the cucumber and cut it into small dice. Mix it with the sour cream and season with salt and pepper. Fill the centre of the mould with the sour cream and cucumber. Serve chilled.

SARDINES

The fresh sardines of the Mediterranean are a delicious fish when freshly grilled or fried. Unfortunately they are seldom available in this country. Tinned sardines, however, are cheap and easily available and can be used for a variety of really good first courses. It often surprises me how seldom they are used in everyday cooking. Do buy the better quality sardines, they only cost a few pennies more and the difference in taste is considerable.

Sardines à l'Estragon

8 sardines
4 slices of white bread
Cooking fat
40 g (1½ oz.) butter
1 tablespoon flour
375 ml (¾ pint) milk
1 small onion
1 teaspoon chopped tarragon (or 1 teaspoon tarragon vinegar)
1 teaspoon lemon juice
1 egg yolk
1 tablespoon cream
Salt and freshly ground black pepper

Drain the sardines. Cut the slices of bread to the size of two sardines. Melt 25 g (1 oz.) butter in a saucepan. Add the flour and mix well. Gradually blend in the milk, stirring continually over a medium flame until the sauce is thick and smooth. Bring to the boil and cook for 2 minutes. Peel and chop the onion and cook it gently until soft in 15 g ($\frac{1}{2}$ oz.) of butter. Add the onion, tarragon and lemon juice to the sauce. Season with salt and pepper. Beat the egg yolk with the cream and stir into the sauce. Cook over a medium flame, stirring briskly, for 3 minutes. Do not boil.

Fry the bread slices until crisp in the fat. Place on a heated dish. Put two sardines on each piece of fried bread. Pour the sauce over the sardines. Serve at once.

Sardines à la Grecque

As a money saver this recipe ranks as four star.

2 tins Portuguese sardines in tomato sauce
3 tablespoons olive oil
1 tablespoon white wine vinegar
1 teaspoon Dijon mustard
1 tablespoon finely chopped parsley
1 tablespoon finely chopped chives
Salt and freshly ground black pepper

Drain off any excess oil from the sardines. Arrange them in a shallow serving dish. Combine the olive oil, white wine vinegar, mustard, parsley, chives and seasoning and mix well. Pour the dressing over the sardines. Serve well chilled with thin slices of buttered brown bread.

Note: A crushed garlic clove can be added to the dressing.

Fried Goujons of Sole

4 fillets of sole
1 beaten egg
Salt and pepper

4 tablespoons breadcrumbs
2 tablespoons olive oil
50 g (2 oz.) butter
Parsley
Sauce tartare (see page 213)

Cut the sole into finger-size strips with kitchen scissors. Dip the fish into the beaten egg, seasoned with salt and pepper, and then into the breadcrumbs. Heat the oil and butter until smoking in a large frying pan. Add the fish and cook until crisp and golden brown. Drain on crumpled kitchen paper. Serve with a garnish of fried sprigs of parsley and sauce tartare.

Note: 'Goujons' are small fish found in the Mediterranean area and are often served in this way.

SQUID OR INKFISH

Many of the larger fishmongers are now selling an American variety of squid. Their taste is not over-exciting, but their smooth, rubbery texture is delicious. In the south and west of England it is sometimes possible to get small octopus but these are not as tender as the squid and should be boiled before being grilled or fried. Squid dipped in a frying batter and deep fried are most delicious, either by themselves or as part of a fritto misto. They can also be grilled or fried with a tomato sauce, but are best of all as a salad, well chilled.

PREPARING SQUID. Gently pull off the head and the ink bag from the pocket-like body. Cut off and reserve the tentacles and discard the rest of the head.

Turn the body inside out and remove the backbone which will slide out easily and looks like a small cellophane dagger. Turn the body the right side out. Rub off the thin purplish skin under cold running water. Cut the body into thin rings, leave the tentacles whole.

Calamari (Squid) Salad

600 g (1½ lb.) squid
Salt and freshly ground black pepper
4 tablespoons olive oil
1 tablespoon lemon juice
½ teaspoon marjoram
1 tablespoon chopped parsley

Prepare the squid as shown above and reserve the tentacles.
Cut the bodies into thin strips. Sprinkle with salt and pepper,
1 tablespoon olive oil, 1 teaspoon lemon juice and the marjoram. Put under a fierce grill for 10 minutes. Leave to cool.
Arrange in a shallow serving dish.

Combine the remaining olive oil and lemon juice with the
chopped parsley. Season with salt and pepper and pour the
dressing over the squid. Chill well before serving.

Note: The squid can be boiled instead of grilled, and
dressed in the same way.

TRUITE AU BLEU

Trout cooked au bleu should be alive 10 minutes before being
put into the water. Most great restaurants have a large tank
with trout swimming around in it for this purpose. Dead trout
can be used but the flavour is not so perfect nor the colour so
beautiful. If dead, the trout must be absolutely fresh. Frozen
fish are not good enough for this dish.

Four 200 g (½ lb.) live trout
3 tablespoons vinegar
1 litre (2 pints) water
125 ml (¼ pint) vinegar
2 tablespoons salt
4 peppercorns
1 bay leaf
1 small onion – peeled and halved
1 sprig parsley

Hollandaise or horseradish sauce (see pages 214 and 219)

10 minutes before cooking, kill the fish with a sharp blow on the head. Gut and clean them. Do not remove the heads or tails and be careful not to damage the scales. Moisten with 3 tablespoons vinegar.

Combine stock ingredients in a large pan. Bring to the boil and cook for 10 minutes. Strain the stock into a clean shallow pan. Slide the trout gently into the stock. Bring to the boil and simmer gently for 6 minutes. Gently remove the fish. Serve the fish hot with a hollandaise or horseradish sauce. To be really correct, the fish should be brought to the table in the stock and served directly from the pan.

Note: The eyes of Truite au Bleu are considered by many to be a great delicacy.

Sole or White Fish in Cider Sauce

8 fillets sole or other white fish
50 g (2 oz.) butter
3 tablespoons chopped parsley
2 tablespoons dry breadcrumbs
250 ml ($\frac{1}{2}$ pint) dry cider
Salt and freshly ground black pepper
4 tablespoons double cream

Butter a shallow baking dish thoroughly with 25 g (1 oz.) butter. Sprinkle with half the parsley. Arrange the fish in the dish. Cover with the remaining parsley and sprinkle with the breadcrumbs. Dot with the remaining butter. Season the cider with salt and pepper and pour it over the fish. Bake the fish in a moderate oven (180 C., 350 F., Reg. 4) for 20 minutes. Pour over the cream and serve at once.

Rose Sole

A cool, pretty summer dish.

8 small fillets sole
1 litre (2 pints) water
125 ml ($\frac{1}{4}$ pint) white wine
1 bay leaf
6 peppercorns
1 sprig parsley
1 teaspoon salt
2 teaspoons lemon juice
125 ml ($\frac{1}{4}$ pint) mayonnaise
1 tablespoon tomato chutney
2 tablespoons cream
1 teaspoon Worcester sauce
Freshly ground black pepper
1 small tin pimento

Combine the water, wine, bay leaf, peppercorns, parsley, salt and 1 teaspoon lemon juice in a shallow pan. Add the fillets to the liquid and bring slowly to the boil. When the liquid boils the fish is cooked. Drain and cool the fillets. Arrange them on a shallow serving dish.

Combine the mayonnaise, tomato chutney, cream, Worcester sauce and 1 teaspoon lemon juice. Mix well and season with pepper. Drain the pimento and chop finely. Mix half the chopped pimento with the sauce and pour over the fillets of sole. Garnish with the rest of the chopped pimento. Serve chilled.

SNAILS (ESCARGOTS)

The best snails come from the vineyards of France. Like oysters they are an acquired taste and since they are always cooked with a large amount of garlic, they are only for those who enjoy a strong garlic flavour. In this country snails are usually bought in tins with the shells separately wrapped but it is sometimes possible to buy them frozen and ready stuffed with a highly flavoured butter. Frozen snails need only be heated in a hot oven until the butter has melted and is bubbling. Should you ever come across fresh snails you must starve them for 48 hours to rid them of any poisons. The day before you want to use them soak the snails in their shells for 24 hours in water with 3 tablespoons coarse salt. Use an earthenware pot with a tight fitting lid or you may find them all over the kitchen!

Boil live snails in a court bouillon (750 ml (1½ pints) water, 125 ml (¼ pint) vinegar, 1 sliced onion, 2 shallots, bouquet garni and salt) for 20 minutes. Drain them well and stuff them with a garlic and herb butter. Allow 6–12 snails per serving depending on what is to follow. Snails should be served on special plates with shaped tongs to hold the snails steady and small two pronged forks to remove the meat from the shells. A good substitute are shallow soup plates and skewers. Supply plenty of French bread to mop up the juices, and a large supply of paper napkins since it is a messy procedure, though worthwhile.

Snails à la Bourguignonne

The most popular way to serve snails.

2–4 dozen snails with separate shells
3 onions
3 cloves garlic
2 tablespoons finely chopped parsley
Salt and freshly ground black pepper
200 g (8 oz.) butter
1 lemon

Peel and chop the onions finely. Put the garlic through a garlic press or pound it to a paste in a pestle and mortar. Work the onions, garlic and parsley into the butter and season well with salt and pepper. Drain the snails and rinse them in cold water. Stuff them into their shells, being careful not to push them down too far. Seal the opening with a teaspoon of the butter mixture. Arrange on special plates or in a shallow baking dish. Heat in a hot oven (220 C., 425 F., Reg. 7) for

10–15 minutes until the butter is bubbling and the snails are hot through.

Serve hot with hot French bread and butter and wedges of lemon.

Truites Aux Amandes

4 fresh 200 g ($\frac{1}{2}$ lb.) trout
125 ml ($\frac{1}{4}$ pint) milk
Flour
Salt and pepper
100 g (4 oz.) butter
100 g (4 oz.) blanched, split almonds
1 teaspoon lemon juice
Quarters of lemon

Clean and gut the fish. Do not remove the head or tails. Dry on a cloth. Dip in the milk and roll in seasoned flour. Heat 50 g (2 oz.) of butter in a frying pan. When the butter is foaming add the trout and cook until golden brown on both sides. Remove the fish onto a heated serving dish and keep warm.

Heat the remaining butter in the same pan. When it is foaming add the split almonds. Cook over a strong heat until the almonds and the butter are brown. Add a teaspoon lemon juice to the almonds and pour them over the fish. Serve hot with quarters of lemon.

Tuna Fish Pâté

1 198 g (7 oz.) tin tuna fish
2 hard boiled eggs
50 g (2 oz.) softened butter
1 tablespoon mixed chopped parsley, chives and tarragon
Salt and freshly ground black pepper
Parsley
Quarters of lemon

Drain the tuna fish to remove all the oil. Put the fish and the eggs through the fine blade of a mincing machine. Add the softened butter and the chopped herbs and mix until well blended. Season with salt and freshly ground black pepper. Shape the mixture into a pyramid on a serving dish and chill well before serving.

Garnish with sprigs of parsley and serve with quarters of lemon and hot toast.

WHITEBAIT

These tiny little fish (often called by their French name blanchaille on restaurant menus) are seldom more than 5 cm (2 inches) long. They are the babies of the herring and are eaten whole, head, tail and all – you try boning them! Whitebait are best bought fresh from a fishmonger but they can be bought frozen, in which case they will need to be very well drained and dried before cooking.

Fried Whitebait

400 g (1 lb.) whitebait
Flour
Salt and pepper
Deep cooking fat or olive oil for frying
Deep fat fryer and basket
8 sprigs of parsley
1 lemon
Sauce tartare (see page 213)

Season the flour with salt and pepper. Toss the whitebait in the flour until it is coated (I do this in a large paper bag). Heat the fat until it smokes. Throw in the whitebait in small quantities and shake the basket so that the fish do not stick together. Cook until golden brown and crisp, about 3 minutes. Drain the fish on crumpled kitchen paper and keep warm while frying the rest. When all the fish are cooked, plunge the parsley in the hot fat for ½ minute. Serve the whitebait garnished with the fried parsley and quarters of lemon. Serve sauce tartare and thin slices of buttered brown bread separately.

Note: Traditionally whitebait should be served on a white napkin.

Whitebait Salad

400 g (1 lb.) whitebait
1 litre (2 pints) water
A sprig of thyme
1 bay leaf
Salt

SAUCE VINAIGRETTE
1 teaspoon mustard
3 tablespoons olive oil
1 tablespoon white wine vinegar
Salt and freshly ground black pepper
1 tablespoon mixed chopped parsley, chives and capers

Bring the water and the herbs to the boil. Add a good pinch of salt. Put in the fish and boil for 1 minute. Drain and cool.

Add a little of the olive oil to the mustard and mix into a smooth paste. Gradually mix in the rest of the oil. Add the vinegar, the chopped parsley, chives and capers and season with salt and plenty of freshly ground black pepper. Pour the sauce vinaigrette over the fish. Serve well chilled with thin slices of buttered brown bread.

Fish au Gratin

This is a basic recipe which can be varied in many ways. It can well be made in advance and re-heated.

500 g (1¼ lbs.) fish fillets (sole, plaice, whiting, etc.)
250 ml (½ pint) milk
25 g (1 oz.) butter
3 tablespoons flour
125 ml (¼ pint) milk
1 egg yolk
1 tablespoon cream
1 tablespoon dry vermouth, sherry or lemon juice
Salt and pepper
2 tablespoons grated Gruyère, Parmesan or Cheddar cheese

Place the fillets in a well buttered baking dish. Pour over 250 ml ($\frac{1}{2}$ pint) milk and cover with buttered paper or aluminium foil. Bake the fish in a moderate oven (180 C., 350 F., Reg. 4) for 10–15 minutes until the fish is tender. Carefully drain the fillets and reserve the liquid.

Melt the butter in a pan. Add the flour and mix well. Gradually mix in the milk used for cooking the fish and an extra 125 ml ($\frac{1}{4}$ pint) milk. Bring to the boil and stir continually until the sauce is thick and smooth. Remove the sauce from the heat. Beat the egg yolk with the cream and blend it into the sauce. Add the vermouth, sherry or lemon juice and season with salt and pepper.

Arrange the fillets in a fireproof serving dish. Pour over the sauce and sprinkle the cheese over the surface. Brown in a hot oven (230 C., 450 F., Reg. 8) for 5–10 minutes. Serve hot.

Variations: Add to the sauce:
1. 100g (4 oz.) peeled prawns
2. 100 g (4 oz.) cooked, sliced mushrooms
3. 2–3 tablespoons tomato purée.

Fish Mousse

300 g ($\frac{3}{4}$ lb.) plaice or sole fillets, or halibut
1 small tin pimento, drained and chopped
250 ml ($\frac{1}{2}$ pint) mayonnaise
125 ml ($\frac{1}{4}$ pint) cream
1 tablespoon tomato ketchup
1 teaspoon Worcester sauce
15 g ($\frac{1}{2}$ oz.) gelatine dissolved in 1 tablespoon hot lemon
   juice
1 egg white
Watercress
French dressing

Steam the fish fillets over boiling water for 15 minutes. Leave to cool and remove any black skin. Flake the fish with a fork. Mix the tomato ketchup and the Worcester sauce with the mayonnaise. Add the fish and the chopped pimento. Stir in the gelatine. Whip the cream and fold it into the fish mixture. Whip the egg white until stiff and fold it into the mixture. Pour into a mould and leave in a refrigerator until set.

Turn out the mould and decorate it with some sprigs of watercress dipped in French dressing. Serve chilled.

Fish Salad

200 g ($\frac{1}{2}$ lb.) cooked fillet of sole or plaice
200 g ($\frac{1}{2}$ lb.) cooked prawns
100 g ($\frac{1}{4}$ lb.) cooked peas
2 firm tomatoes, sliced
1 lettuce
125 ml ($\frac{1}{4}$ pint) mayonnaise
1 tin anchovies

Arrange the fish, prawns, peas and sliced tomatoes on a bed of lettuce leaves. Spoon over the mayonnaise and garnish with a few anchovies.

Variations:
1. Hard boiled eggs, asparagus or beetroot can be used instead of the peas and tomatoes.
2. 1 tablespoon tomato purée can be added to the mayonnaise.

Good Friday Salad

600 g (1$\frac{1}{2}$ lb.) turbot or halibut
200 g ($\frac{1}{2}$ lb.) peeled prawns
1 large onion
2 tablespoons chopped parsley
$\frac{1}{2}$ tablespoon chopped capers
6 tablespoons olive oil
3 tablespoons lemon juice
Salt and freshly ground black pepper
1 lettuce (optional)

Steam the turbot or halibut in a steamer over just boiling

water. Cook until just tender, 20–30 minutes (the fish is cooked when it just comes off the bone). Remove any bones or skin from the fish and flake it with a fork. Peel and chop the onion. Combine the fish, prawns, onion, parsley and capers. Mix the olive oil with the lemon juice. Season generously with salt and freshly ground black pepper. Pour the dressing over the fish whilst the fish is still warm. Leave to cool and chill before serving.

The fish can be served on lettuce leaves on individual plates. Accompany with hot garlic bread (see page 227).

CHAPTER SIX

SMOKED FISH

There is a wide variety of smoked fish on the market. Some are in the luxury class but others like the kipper are within anyone's means. Smoked salmon and smoked eel are delicious but so are many of the cheaper fish which, with a little imagination, can be made into delectable first courses.

When buying smoked fish watch out for any dryness – a good indication of poor quality. If smoked fish is exposed to the air or to heat for any length of time, it loses condition and although rubbing with a little olive oil will help to combat the dryness, it will never again be perfect. Keep smoked fish in a cool place or a refrigerator wrapped in cling wrapping or greaseproof paper. Mackerel, buckling and trout should be skinned before being served.

Smoked Buckling Salad

4 buckling (6 if they are small ones)
1 lettuce
2 boiled potatoes
1 apple
1 onion
3 tablespoons olive oil
1 tablespoon vinegar
Salt and pepper
1 lemon
Dill

Skin and fillet the buckling. Arrange the fillets on lettuce leaves on 4 plates. Dice the potatoes. Peel, core and dice the apple. Chop the onion. Combine the olive oil and vinegar and season with salt and pepper. Mix with the potatoes, apples and onion. Arrange the salad around the buckling fillets. Garnish with wedges of lemon and with dill.

Taramasalata

A classic Turkish and Greek pâté made from smoked cod's roe. Making the pâté is rather like making mayonnaise. An emulsion is formed by beating oil slowly into the cod's roe, until a smooth creamy paste results. Smoked cod's roe can be bought fresh from fishmongers or in pots or jars. Fresh cod's roe has a tough skin which must be removed.

200 g (8 oz.) smoked cod's roe
5 slices white bread
250 ml ($\frac{1}{2}$ pint) cold water
1 small onion
250 ml ($\frac{1}{2}$ pint) olive oil
4 tablespoons lemon juice
Freshly ground black pepper

Remove any tough skin from the roe. Soak the bread in the water until soft. Squeeze out excess water. Combine the bread and cod's roe in a pestle and mortar. Pound until a smooth paste is formed. Turn into a bowl. Peel and grate the onion, add to the cod's roe. Beat the onion into the paste with a wire whisk. Add half the oil, drop by drop, beating all the time. Then add the lemon juice a little at a time alternating with the rest of the oil. Continue to beat until the mixture is a light creamy paste. Season with plenty of black pepper. Pile the mixture in a dish and chill.

Serve with green olives, black olives, radishes and plenty of hot toast and butter.

Note: If you feel the taramasalata has rather too strong a taste, add a tablespoon of yoghurt after the oil and lemon juice.

Smoked Eel

Unfortunately this smooth textured delicacy is prohibitively expensive. Good delicatessen stores sell it in fillets or on the bone, when it needs to be skinned and filleted. The flesh is oily and very rich. It should be served on a bed of crisp lettuce leaves with quarters of lemon and thin slices of buttered brown bread. Allow 50 g (2 oz.) of filleted smoked eel for each serving.

In Sweden I have had smoked eel served with scrambled eggs – a delicious and very satisfying luncheon dish.

Kipper (poor man's smoked salmon)

2 large kippers
1 onion
2 tablespoons olive oil
2 tablespoons lemon juice
Freshly ground black pepper
1 lettuce

Remove the kipper meat from the bones in bite size pieces. Put them in a dish. Peel the onion, chop it finely and sprinkle over the kipper. Combine the lemon juice and the olive oil, season with pepper and pour over the kippers. Leave to marinade for at least an hour, drain well.

Arrange the kippers on crisp lettuce leaves on four plates. Serve cold with thin slices of buttered brown bread.

Kipper Pâté

This is a most unusual pâté. Inexpensive to make and yet with luxury in the taste.

125 g (5 oz.) kipper fillets
Juice of ½ lemon
75 g (3 oz.) softened butter

2 teaspoons finely chopped parsley
2 teaspoons tomato purée
Freshly ground black pepper
Mace

Dot the kipper fillets with a little butter, cover with tin foil and bake in a moderate oven (180 C., 350 F., Reg. 4) for 20 minutes. Cool. Rub the kipper through a fine sieve or food mill, or purée in an electric liquidizer. Add the lemon juice and mix well until smooth. Blend in the softened butter, the parsley and the tomato purée. Season with freshly ground black pepper and a pinch of mace. Pack the pâté in a jar and chill. Serve with hot toast.

Smoked Mackerel

The oily flesh of the mackerel responds well to smoking and they are much cheaper than smoked trout or salmon. Depending on the smoking process, they can be served either hot or cold. I prefer to fillet the fish before serving.

Smoked mackerel are served with quarters of lemon, horseradish sauce and thin slices of buttered brown bread and they make an excellent pâté; purée the boned flesh and combine it with whipped cream and seasonings.

Smoked Oysters

These are only obtainable in tins, packed in oil. They are useful to serve as part of a mixed hors d'oeuvres and also on cocktail sticks with drinks.

SMOKED SALMON

Smoked salmon is among the princes of first courses. I have included a number of recipes using smoked salmon but it is best served by itself. Slicing smoked salmon is an arduous task and not to be attempted unless you have unlimited time and patience. Any fishmonger or delicatessen store that sells smoked salmon will cut it for you.

The best smoked salmon is our own Scottish or Tamar.

The Norwegian and Canadian salmon are much cheaper but inclined to be dry and salty. It can also be bought ready sliced, in polythene packs which are ideal for the made up dishes. For a large party a whole side of smoked salmon can be bought at a wholesale price from a number of fishmongers, but you have to be prepared to cut it yourself. For cocktail recipes, and dishes requiring chopped smoked salmon, trimmings can be bought at a very reasonable price.

Choose smoked salmon that has a good orange pink colour and an oily sheen. If it is dry, wipe it over with a cloth soaked in olive oil.

Plain Smoked Salmon

50g (2 oz.) smoked salmon per person
Lemon quarters
Buttered brown bread

Have the smoked salmon cut into wafer thin slices. Serve on individual plates with a quarter of lemon to each serving. Accompany with thinly cut slices of buttered brown bread. Have a pepper mill and cayenne pepper on the table.

Smoked Salmon Rolls with Cream and Anchovies

200 g (8 oz.) smoked salmon
250 ml ($\frac{1}{2}$ pint) double cream
Juice of $\frac{1}{2}$ lemon
Pepper
1 bunch watercress
1 small tin anchovy fillets

Cut the salmon into rectangular pieces about 10 cm (four inches) by 5 cm (two inches). Reserve the trimmings. Whip the cream until stiff. Mix the lemon juice into the cream. Season with pepper. Cut the stalks off the watercress. Chop the leaves. Drain the anchovies well and chop them. Mix the watercress and anchovies into the cream.

Place a spoonful of the mixture on each slice of salmon.

Roll up carefully into neat rolls. Chop the salmon trimmings and mix them with the remaining cream mixture. Pile this in the centre of a serving dish. Arrange the rolls around the edge. Garnish with watercress and serve chilled with thin slices of buttered brown bread.

Smoked Salmon and Egg Mousse

4 hard boiled eggs
100 g ($\frac{1}{4}$ lb.) smoked salmon
375 ml ($\frac{3}{4}$ pint) mayonnaise
1$\frac{1}{4}$ tablespoons gelatine
Salt and black pepper
1 tablespoon tomato ketchup
250 ml ($\frac{1}{2}$ pint) whipped double cream
Watercress

Dissolve the gelatine in 2 tablespoons hot water. Chop the hard boiled eggs very finely. Cut the smoked salmon into small strips with kitchen scissors. Add the eggs and smoked salmon to the mayonnaise. Mix in the tomato ketchup.

Fold the gelatine into the mayonnaise mixture. Season with salt and pepper. Fold in the whipped cream. Pour into a wet ring mould and leave in a cool place to set. Turn out and fill the centre of the ring with chopped watercress.

Smoked Salmon with Scrambled Eggs

I have had this often in Scandinavia as a luncheon dish, but it also makes a good first course before a cold main course. Most delicatessen stores sell smoked salmon trimmings which are ideal for a dish of this sort.

5 eggs
100 g ($\frac{1}{4}$ lb.) smoked salmon
Salt and freshly ground black pepper
2 tablespoons cream
40 g (1$\frac{1}{2}$ oz.) butter
Cayenne pepper
1 tablespoon chopped parsley

Beat the eggs lightly. Season with salt and freshly ground black pepper. Add the chopped smoked salmon. Stir in the cream. Melt the butter in a saucepan. When it is foaming, but not coloured, pour in the eggs. Cook over a low heat, stirring occasionally until the eggs are cooked but not dry.

Garnish with chopped parsley and a dusting of cayenne pepper. Serve with triangles of freshly toasted bread.

Smoked Trout Pâté

Smoked trout is readily available from good delicatessen stores and is a lot cheaper than smoked salmon. Choose trout that have a good oily sheen to their skin.

1 good sized smoked trout
75 g (3 oz.) butter
Salt, pepper and mace
Lemon juice
1 lemon

Skin the trout and remove the head, tail and bones. Pound the flesh until smooth in a pestle and mortar or rub through a hair sieve. Soften the butter and work it into the trout. Season with salt, pepper, mace and a little lemon juice. Pack into a jar or a shallow bowl. Chill before serving. Serve with quarters of lemon and freshly made toast.

Note: This also makes a good sandwich filling.

CHAPTER SEVEN

SHELLFISH

Like smoked fish, shellfish come in many varieties and prices, ranging from cockles and winkles as the cheapest, to oysters as the most expensive. With the improvement of cold storage and freezing more exotic shellfish are appearing on the market every year. In some London shops one can now buy freshly boiled small scampi tails (delicious with mayonnaise, served in their shells) and even king crabs and clams from America.

It is most important that all shellfish should be fresh, since some of the most virulent forms of food poisoning are caused by shellfish gone bad. If you have any doubts about freshness when buying shellfish from a fishmonger, do not hesitate to give it a good sniff – fresh shellfish have virtually no smell except that of the sea but they quickly develop one if they are not in prime condition. Oysters and mussels, unless they have been preserved, should be bought alive and only from reputable fishmongers. If you have to keep them for a few hours cover them with salt water and feed them with a handful of oatmeal.

All forms of shellfish make good first courses. I once had a really delicious dinner starting with winkles heated in a garlic and parsley batter. On the whole I would say that most shellfish are best of all served *au naturel* with lemon juice or mayonnaise but of course they go further if used in made up dishes.

CRAB
In Great Britain we have a rather disappointing crab population consisting of only one main variety. In hotter climates

there are other, more delicious, species such as soft shell crabs, black crabs and hermit crabs. Like lobsters, crabs should be eaten when absolutely fresh and soon after being boiled. They can be used to make many of the lobster and prawn dishes, but the most popular way of serving crab is to have it dressed in its shell. Buy crabs that have large claws and are relatively heavy for their size.

COOKING CRABS. In England it is usual for a fishmonger to sell crabs ready cooked. Should you have a fresh crab, plunge it head first into a boiling court bouillon consisting of a litre (quart) of water, 125 ml ($\frac{1}{4}$ pint) white wine, 1 onion cut in half, 5 peppercorns, 1 teaspoon salt, 1 bay leaf, 1 sprig parsley. Cook for 15 minutes to the pound and cool the crabs in the liquid.

Crabs have a poisonous stomach sac which must be carefully removed.

TO PREPARE CRABS. Boil the crabs and leave until cool. Twist off the legs and claws. Place the crab on its back with the tail flap (the bit to which the legs are attached) facing you. Place your thumbs under the tail flap and push firmly upwards until the body comes away from the shell. Carefully remove the mouth and the stomach sac. The mouth is situated in the shell. It is a spiky piece of shell with the white stomach sac, usually filled with a fibrous substance, attached to it. Discard also any soft green substance that is in the shell, and the spongy, feathery fingers – the gills, on the sides of the shell – romantically called 'dead men's fingers'. Remove all the meat from the inside of the shell. Keep the brown meat separate from the white. Trim round the paler outside edges of the shell with a sharp knife or tough scissors, leaving a natural open serving dish. Twist off the first joints of the claws and break the shells with a hammer. Remove all the meat from the claws.

Dressed Crab

4 small freshly cooked crabs
1 teaspoon English mustard
1 tablespoon olive oil
1 teaspoon lemon juice
1 tablespoon cream
Salt and black pepper
1 hard boiled egg
2 teaspoons finely chopped parsley

Discard the mouth and the stomach sac of the crabs. Remove all the meat from the shell and the claws of the crabs, keeping the brown and the white meat separate. Combine the mustard, olive oil, lemon juice and cream. Mix the dressing with the brown meat. Season well with salt and freshly ground black pepper. Arrange the brown meat in the centre of the crab shell. Arrange the white meat around the edge. Separate the yolk from the white of the hard boiled egg. Chop the white finely, sieve the yolk. Sprinkle the egg over the surface of the crab. Finish with a dusting of chopped parsley.

Serve the crab chilled with mayonnaise or French dressing made with mustard.

Crab Mousse

1 large tin crab or 200 g ($\frac{1}{2}$ lb.) fresh or frozen crab
1 tablespoon aspic jelly crystals
250 ml ($\frac{1}{2}$ pint) warm water
2 tablespoons brandy
250 ml ($\frac{1}{2}$ pint) double cream
Salt and freshly ground black pepper
Cayenne pepper
1 teaspoon finely chopped parsley
1 lemon

Drain the crab and mash the meat well with a fork or press it through a sieve. Dissolve the aspic jelly in the warm water and mix it with the brandy and the crab. Season with salt, freshly ground black pepper and a pinch of cayenne. Whip the cream until stiff. Fold the cream into the crab with the parsley. Pour into a serving bowl and chill for at least 2 hours. Garnish with parsley.

Serve cold with hot toast and quarters of lemon.

Potted Crab

200 g ($\frac{1}{2}$ lb.) crabmeat
75 g (3 oz.) butter
Salt and freshly ground black pepper
$\frac{1}{2}$ teaspoon mace
1 lemon

Make sure that the crabmeat is free from any bones or fibres. Melt 50 g (2 oz.) of butter in a heavy pan. Add the crabmeat and seasoning. Cook over a low heat for 5 minutes without browning. Cool and pack in a small jar or terrine. Melt the remaining butter and heat it until it foams – do not allow it to brown. Strain the butter through a muslin cloth and pour it over the crab. Leave to set. Serve with quarters of lemon and hot toast.

Note: Potted crab may be kept for 7–10 days in a refrigerator.

Crawfish (*Langouste or Spiny Lobster*)

These neolithic, well-armoured creatures resemble ugly squat lobsters. They have no claws but carry more flesh than a lobster of the same size. The flesh is richer than that of the lobster but is inclined to be tough in the larger varieties. Crawfish are killed and cooked in the same way as lobsters and can be used for all lobster dishes. Only small crawfish should be served *au naturel*.

LOBSTERS

On the Continent it is illegal to sell pregnant female lobsters. Unfortunately this is not the case in this country and as a result these succulent armoured creatures are becoming harder to get and more expensive. Ideally one should buy lobsters alive, when they are still a dark blue black colour and when a vicious plunge of their claws can do you a nasty injury.

If you buy your lobsters from a fishmonger, they will undoubtedly be boiled. In this case there are two good ways of telling whether they are freshly cooked. 1. A fresh lobster will have its tail curved under it. The tail will still be supple and on being pulled out and released, will return to its former position. 2. A freshly boiled lobster is heavy relative to its size. A large lobster that feels light will have dried out inside its shell and will be tough and tasteless.

Female lobsters are rather more tasty and tender than the male of the species. They are broader across the tail and have thinner front feet. Small lobsters, 200–400 g ($\frac{1}{2}$–1 lb.), are more succulent than the larger ones. Lobsters over 1·5 kg (3 lbs.) are inclined to be tough.

COOKING LOBSTERS. The arguments on painless lobster killing go on for ever. Many great cooks recommend the sharp instrument method and use this before boiling. I kill them this way for dishes requiring an uncooked lobster, but for all other recipes I kill the lobsters by plunging them head first into boiling water. The R.S.P.C.A. have assured me that they die immediately they hit the water and that all subsequent movements are a result of reflexes.

To kill lobsters before cooking them
1. Insert a sharp pointed knife across the point where the tail and body join, thus severing the spinal cord.
2. Insert a sharp pointed skewer through the shell at a point in the centre of the head just behind the eyes, thus piercing the brain.

I find the first method more successful, as aiming a skewer

at a small point on an excited live lobster is no easy matter and the shells are sometimes incredibly tough. Lobsters must be cooked as soon as they have been killed.

BOILING LOBSTERS. To each litre (quart) of water add 125 ml ($\frac{1}{4}$ pint) of white wine, 1 onion cut in half, 5 peppercorns, 1 teaspoon salt, 1 bay leaf, 1 sprig parsley. Combine enough water to cover the lobsters with the wine and other ingredients. Bring to the boil and when it is boiling fast plunge the live lobsters head first into the water. Hold them across the back just behind the claws. If there is more than one lobster, allow the water to return to the boil after adding each one. Cover and cook for 15–30 minutes according to size. Leave to cool in the liquid.

TO PREPARE LOBSTERS FOR EATING. Stretch the lobster out flat on a wooden board, tummy side down. Remove the claws by twisting them sharply. Use a strong sharp knife and insert it firmly into the shell. Drive the knife down the centre of the shell and divide it neatly into two. Remove the stomach sac – a small circular bag situated in the head and usually filled with a fibre-like substance – and the thin black line of intestine which stretches the length of the tail. Crack the claws with a hammer wrapped in a cloth or a pair of nutcrackers.

FROZEN LOBSTERS. Frozen lobsters are not suitable for serving *au naturel* unless they have been frozen at a very low temperature. They are however perfectly adequate for hot lobster dishes and for cocktails and salads.

TINNED LOBSTER. Tinned lobster is expensive and very disappointing in comparison with the real thing. Use tinned lobster only in emergencies and where lobster is used in a sauce or merely as an addition to other ingredients.

Half Lobster in the Shell

Lobster is a rich and filling fish and as a first course I feel one should only serve the small ones. Nothing is more delicious than a really fresh small and tender half lobster resting on a bed of crisp lettuce leaves and nothing more unpalatable than one that is oversized, dry and indigestible.

2 small cooked lobsters
1 lettuce
Mayonnaise

Using a very sharp strong knife, cut the lobsters neatly down the centre and remove the stomach sac and the black line of intestine stretching the length of the shell fish. Detach the large claws and crush each one carefully with a hammer or other suitable instrument. Arrange each half lobster with one claw on a bed of lettuce leaves. Chill before serving and accompany with thin slices of brown bread and butter and a mayonnaise made with lemon juice instead of vinegar. Eating lobster like this is a messy business so provide finger bowls, if you have them, and adequate napkins.

Lobster Salad

The only real reason for serving lobster salad instead of lobsters in their shells is economy. While you need two small lobsters for a first course for four people, if they are served in their shells, one medium lobster will provide an ample first course if it is served as a salad.

1 medium cooked lobster
2 lettuce hearts
2 hard boiled eggs
250 ml ($\frac{1}{2}$ pint) mayonnaise
2 tomatoes
$\frac{1}{4}$ cucumber
6 stoned olives
4 anchovies

Cut the lobster neatly down the back and remove the stomach sac and intestine. Remove all the meat from the shell and claws and cut into neat pieces about 2·5 cm (1 inch) across.

Arrange the lobster and quartered hard boiled eggs on the lettuce hearts. Dot it with the mayonnaise and garnish with thin slices of tomato, cucumber, the olives and the anchovies. Serve chilled.

Potted Lobster

200 g ($\frac{1}{2}$ lb.) cooked lobster meat
75 g (3 oz.) butter
Salt and freshly ground black pepper
$\frac{1}{2}$ teaspoon mace
1 lemon

Chop the lobster into small dice. Melt 50 g (2 oz.) butter in a heavy pan. Add the lobster and seasoning and cook over a low heat for 5 minutes without browning. Cool and pack into a jar or small terrine.

Melt the remaining butter and heat until it foams – do not allow to brown. Strain the butter through a muslin cloth and pour over the lobster. The lobster should be completely covered. If necessary melt and strain over some more butter. Serve with quarters of lemon and hot toast.

Note: Potted lobster may be kept for 7–10 days in a refrigerator.

Lobster Thermidor

2 freshly boiled lobsters (300–400 g ($\frac{3}{4}$–1 lb.) each)
50 g (2 oz.) butter
50 g (2 oz.) flour
125 ml ($\frac{1}{4}$ pint) milk
Salt, and paprika pepper
A pinch of cayenne pepper
2 egg yolks
1 tablespoon cream
2 tablespoons sherry
2 tablespoons dry breadcrumbs

Split the lobsters down the back. Remove the stomach sac and the thin black line of the intestine. Split the claws and remove the meat. Remove and discard the legs. Remove all the meat from the body, being careful not to break or damage the shells. Cut all the meat into small dice. Melt 25 g (1 oz.) butter in a saucepan. Cook the lobster meat in the butter, over a medium heat, for 3 minutes. Keep warm. Melt 15 g (½ oz.) butter in another saucepan. Add the flour and mix well. Gradually add the milk, stirring continually until the sauce is thick and smooth. Pour the sauce over the lobster meat and cook for a further 2 minutes over a low heat. Season with salt, paprika and a pinch of cayenne. Remove the sauce from the heat. Beat the egg yolks with the cream and sherry. Add to the lobster and mix well. Fill the lobster shells with this mixture. Sprinkle the breadcrumbs over the surface and dot with 15 g (½ oz.) butter. Bake the lobsters in a fairly hot oven (200 C., 400 F., Reg. 6) for 5–8 minutes until brown. Or brown under a medium hot grill. Serve hot.

Lobster thermidor is a very rich and filling dish and should only be served before a light main course.

MUSSELS

Mussels in their natural state need more preparation for cooking than any other shellfish. I think they are well worth the trouble and I never grudge the hours I spend at the sink, scrubbing the shells clean. They can be served in a great variety of ways. Allow 8–10 or 250 ml (½ pint) mussels per portion.

FRESH MUSSELS. Discard any mussels that are open. Leave the mussels soaking in fresh clean water until you can clean them. Scrub the shells under cold running water to remove all the mud, sand and seaweed, etc. If the mussels are very dirty a wire brush is useful for this job. Using a small sharp knife, pluck out the 'beard' (a protruding wiry growth from the side of the mussel). The mussels are now ready to cook.

MUSSELS BOUGHT FROM A FISHMONGER. The arduous scraping and cleaning job is done for you by the fishmonger and it is only necessary to rinse the shells in cold water and check that none of them are open. Mussels are sold by the pint.

BOTTLED MUSSELS. Most varieties of bottled mussels sold in this country are packed in vinegar and are not suitable for the following recipes. A few brands pack mussels in water and these, although nothing like as tasty as fresh ones, can be used in most of the dishes.

TINNED MUSSELS. On the whole very superior to the bottled variety as they are packed in brine. The best I have found are of Danish origin and they make a good alternative to fresh shellfish in dishes which do not require the shells.

Moules à La Bordelaise

1·75 litres (4 pints) or 30–40 mussels
125 ml ($\frac{1}{4}$ pint) dry white wine
4 small onions or shallots
2 tablespoons parsley
15 g ($\frac{1}{2}$ oz.) butter
1 tablespoon flour
1 tablespoon tomato paste or purée
Salt and pepper

Scrub the mussels under cold running water. Remove the beards. Place in a large saucepan. Pour over the wine. Cover with a clean cloth and cook over a medium heat until the mussels have opened (6–8 minutes). *Discard any that have not opened.* Remove the empty shells and keep the mussels warm. Strain the liquid through a thin sieve.

Mince the onions and parsley, or chop very finely. Melt the butter in a saucepan. Add the flour and mix well. Gradually blend in half the mussel liquid, stirring continually until smooth. Add the minced onions and parsley and blend in the tomato paste. Season with salt and pepper and cook over a low heat for 10 minutes. Stir in the remainder of the mussel liquid. The sauce should now be the density of thin cream. If it is too thick, thin it with equal quantities of wine and water. Pour the sauce over the mussels and serve hot.

Mussel Paella

Adding rice to this dish makes it a hearty one. Serve mussels in this way only before a light main course.

2 large onions
3 tomatoes
$\frac{1}{2}$ green pepper
1–2 cloves garlic
125 ml ($\frac{1}{4}$ pint) olive oil
50 g (2 oz.) long grain rice
Salt and freshly ground pepper
2 tablespoons chopped parsley
1·5 litres (3 pints) or about 24 mussels

Peel and chop the onions and the tomatoes. Seed and core the pepper and cut the flesh into thin slivers. Press the garlic through a garlic press or mince finely. Heat the oil in a saucepan. Add the rice, onions, garlic, tomatoes and pepper. Season well with salt and pepper. Cover the pan and cook slowly for 15 minutes, stirring occasionally to prevent the rice from sticking. Add the parsley to the rice and mix well. Re-cover and continue to cook over a low heat for a further 15 minutes.

Scrub the mussels under cold running water. Remove the beards. Place in a large saucepan, cover with a cloth and cook over a low heat for 6–8 minutes until they have opened. *Discard any that have not opened.* Remove the empty top shells of the mussels and reserve the liquid in the pan.

Place the rice in a large serving dish. Arrange the mussels on the rice and pour over the liquid from the pan.

Mussel Salad

1·75 litres (4 pints) or 30–40 mussels
1 chopped onion
A sprig of parsley
125 ml ($\frac{1}{4}$ pint) dry white wine or water
100 g (4 oz.) rice
3 tablespoons olive oil
1 tablespoon vinegar
Salt and freshly ground black pepper
2 tablespoons chopped chives

Scrub the mussels under cold running water. Remove the beards from the shells. Place in a large pan with the onion, parsley and white wine or water. Cook for 6–8 minutes over a medium heat, until the mussels have opened. *Discard any that do not open.* Drain and leave to cool.

Cook the rice in boiling water until tender – about 20 minutes. Drain and rinse with cold water. Combine the olive oil and vinegar and pour it over the rice. Remove the mussels from their shells. Add them to the rice and mix gently. Season well with salt and freshly ground black pepper. Arrange in a serving dish and garnish with chopped chives. Chill before serving.

OYSTERS

I consider that oysters should really be eaten raw, rather than cooked, with just a squeeze of lemon juice, a touch of freshly ground black pepper and plenty of brown bread and butter. But for the benefit of those who do not share my views, I have included some of the classic recipes for cooked oysters.

OPENING AND SERVING OYSTERS. Oysters must be fresh and alive when they are eaten or cooked. Preferably they should be eaten within 24 hours of being caught, but if necessary they can be kept for 2–3 days if they are well chilled and tightly packed. Rapid change in temperature quickly kills them and the results of eating a bad oyster are both painful and dangerous. When buying oysters from a fishmonger, keep a look-out for any that have open shells. If the oyster doesn't close its shell at once when tapped lightly it is not safe to eat. In the same way the oyster is liable to be dead if the shell opens too easily or doesn't retract slightly when touched. If there is any doubt, discard the oyster.

Opening oysters is a difficult and often rather dangerous task for the amateur. If possible get your fishmonger or someone who knows what they are doing to do the job. If you have to open the shells yourself, use a sharp strong knife with a rounded end. Hold the oyster in your left hand which should be wrapped in a cloth. Plunge the knife quickly into the hinge at the widest side of the shell. Turn the knife until the shell is forced open and through the muscle which holds the two shells together. Discard the flat shell and slide the knife under the oyster to loosen it from the shell. Try to reserve as much juice as possible. The opening should be done as shortly as possible before the oysters are to be eaten.

Serve oysters on beds of crushed ice on oyster dishes or shallow plates. Accompany with quarters of lemon and slices of buttered brown bread. Tabasco sauce and black and red pepper should also be on the table. Raw oysters are eaten with a fork and 6–12 per person should be allowed, depending on their size and on what is to follow.

Oysters Mornay

6 oysters per serving (Portuguese oysters are ideal for this
  dish)
25 g (1 oz.) butter
25 g (1 oz.) flour
125 ml ($\frac{1}{4}$ pint) milk
2 tablespoons double cream

2 tablespoons grated Gruyère cheese
Salt and pepper

Remove the oysters from their shells and simmer them in their own juice for 30 seconds. Drain well and reserve the juice. Melt the butter in a saucepan. Add the flour and mix well. Gradually stir in the milk and cook slowly until the sauce is thick and smooth. Add the cream and the cheese and season with salt and pepper. Add the oyster juice and cook for 5 minutes over a low heat. Arrange the oysters in individual ramekin dishes and pour over the sauce. Reheat in a very hot oven (240 C., 475 F., Reg. 9) for 5 minutes until the top is golden and bubbling.

Serve at once.

Panned Oysters

24 oysters
1 egg
1 tablespoon olive oil
Salt and pepper
Fine dry breadcrumbs
200 g (8 oz.) flour
1 lemon
Sauce tartare (see page 213)

Remove the oysters from their shells. Mix together the egg and olive oil. Beat well and season with salt and pepper. Roll the oysters in the flour. Dip them in the egg mixture and then coat them with breadcrumbs. Arrange the oysters in a shallow baking dish and cook in a medium oven (190 C, 375 F., Reg. 5) for 15 minutes until golden brown. Serve at once, garnished with quarters of lemon and with sauce tartare.

PRAWNS
Prawns should be cooked as soon as they are caught. They are dropped into boiling water and removed as soon as they

turn bright pink. Fishmongers sell cooked prawns in their shells or ready peeled. To peel prawns break off the heads and the tails and gently remove the shell from the body. Fresh prawns are stiff and brightly coloured, ones in bad condition are flabby and dull looking.

Serve freshly boiled prawns *au naturel* in a glass bowl resting on a bed of ice, accompany them with a mayonnaise and thin slices of buttered brown bread. Peeled prawns can be used in many composite dishes and instead of lobster or crab in many cases. They are useful for garnishing and for adding to many of the dishes included in a selection of hors d'oeuvre.

Spanish Prawns with Garlic

This is a delightful dish for those who like garlic. Serve the prawns in fireproof ramekin dishes.

300 g (12 oz.) peeled prawns
4 large cloves garlic
6 tablespoons olive oil
6 drops Tabasco sauce
1 tablespoon chopped parsley

Peel the garlic cloves and chop them very, very finely – this is important. Heat the olive oil in a saucepan. Add the garlic and cook over a medium heat until the garlic is soft and transparent – about 5 minutes. Add the prawns and the Tabasco sauce. Cook over a medium heat for 5 minutes, shaking the pan frequently.

Divide the prawns and oil between 4 hot fireproof ramekin dishes. Sprinkle the chopped parsley over the surface. Serve piping hot with plenty of hot French bread. Have a pepper mill on the table and encourage your guests to mop up the oil with their bread.

Prawn Toast

300 g (12 oz.) peeled prawns
1 teaspoon cornflour
1 teaspoon ground ginger
1 teaspoon sherry
1 egg white
2 tablespoons minced ham
2 tablespoons finely chopped spring onions
Salt and pepper
8 slices bread
Olive oil

Chop the prawns finely. Mix the cornflour, ginger, sherry and egg white to a smooth paste. Mix in the chopped prawns, ham and spring onions. Season with salt and pepper.

Trim the edges off the bread. Spread each slice with the prawn paste. Press the paste firmly into the bread. Heat some olive oil in a frying pan. Place the bread slices, paste side down in the hot oil and fry until golden brown. Gently turn the slices over and cook until crisp on the other side. Serve at once.

Prawn Cocktail

One of the classic restaurant hors d'oeuvres. It can be made with chopped lobster, chopped Dublin Bay prawns, or crab-meat in the place of the prawns.

300 g (12 oz.) peeled prawns
2 teaspoons lemon juice
Tabasco sauce
Freshly ground black pepper
2 lettuce hearts
1 pint mayonnaise
2 tablespoons tomato ketchup
2 tablespoons cream
A few drops Worcester sauce
Lemon slices

Pour the lemon juice over the prawns. Sprinkle them with a few drops of Tabasco sauce and some freshly ground black pepper. Leave to marinade in a cold place for ½ hour. Shred the lettuce and arrange it in the bottom of 4 glass goblets or glass dishes. Blend the tomato ketchup and cream into the mayonnaise. Flavour with a few drops of Worcester sauce. Arrange the prawns on the shredded lettuce. Pour over the dressing.

Serve chilled with a thin slice of lemon and plenty of thinly sliced brown bread and butter.

Potted Prawns

200 g (½ lb.) peeled and picked prawns
Salt and freshly ground black pepper
75g (3 oz.) butter
½ teaspoon ground mace
1 lemon

Melt 2 oz. butter in a heavy pan. Add the prawns and seasoning and cook them over a low heat for 5 minutes without browning. Cool and pack into a jar or small terrine. Melt the remaining butter and heat until it foams – do not allow it to brown. Strain it through a muslin cloth and pour it over the prawns. The prawns should be completely covered. If necessary pour over more strained butter. Serve with quarters of lemon and hot toast.

Note: Potted prawns will keep for 7–10 days in a refrigerator.

Prawn Salad

200 g (8 oz.) peeled prawns
1 apple
2 sticks celery
125 ml (¼ pint) mayonnaise
Lettuce leaves
1 tablespoon chopped chives or parsley

Peel, core and dice the apple. Slice the celery. Mix the prawns, apple and celery with the mayonnaise and arrange the salad on the lettuce leaves on a shallow serving dish or individual plates. Sprinkle chopped chives or parsley over the top and chill before serving.

SCALLOPS

These delicate fine-textured shellfish are usually bought ready prepared for cooking from the fishmonger. Watch out for a thin black line of intestine which encircles the white part of the fish. Remove it if it is still there. For most dishes the white part of the scallop is chopped and the pink part left whole.

Scallops are usually prepared in a cream sauce and can be served in their own shells. The upper shell is much deeper and more dish-like than the lower shell. Most fishmongers will supply you with these deep shells when you buy the scallops. Allow 2 scallops per serving.

Coquilles St Jacques

8 scallops and shells
1 finely chopped small onion
100 g ($\frac{1}{4}$ lb.) mushrooms
1 large tomato
75 g (3 oz.) butter
25 g (1 oz.) flour
125 ml ($\frac{1}{4}$ pint) milk
Salt, pepper and a pinch of paprika
1 tablespoon chopped parsley

Wash the scallops and clean off the shells. Remove the black vein from the side of the scallops. Place them in a saucepan covered with cold water. Bring to the boil and simmer for 6 minutes. Drain well. Chop the white part but leave the pink whole. Wash and thinly slice the mushrooms. Peel, seed and chop the tomatoes. Melt 50 g (2 oz.) butter in a heavy pan. Add the scallops, onion, tomatoes and mushrooms and fry for 5 minutes over a medium flame.

Melt 25 g (1 oz.) butter in a saucepan, add the flour and stir well over a medium heat until the mixture forms a ball and leaves the sides of the pan. Mix in the milk stirring continually until the sauce is thick and smooth. Add the scallops and the other ingredients to the sauce. Season with salt, pepper and a pinch of paprika. Fill the scallop shells with the hot mixture. Place them under a hot grill for 2 minutes to brown the surface. Sprinkle with chopped parsley before serving.

SCAMPI OR DUBLIN BAY PRAWNS

These are the frozen tails of Dublin Bay prawns or langoustines. They should be defrosted slowly and cooked very gently since it takes little to turn them tough and leathery. Scampi should be used within 12 hours of being defrosted and since they are inclined to be rather watery, they don't really adapt well to being fried in batter or grilled.

Scampi Salad

200 g ($\frac{1}{2}$ lb.) defrosted scampi
2 lettuce hearts
250 ml ($\frac{1}{2}$ pint) mayonnaise
1 teaspoon Worcester sauce
1 tablespoon tomato ketchup
1 lemon

Separate the scampi and steam them until they are pale pink and tender, about 10 minutes. Leave them to cool. Cut each lettuce heart into four and arrange them in a serving bowl. Mound the scampi in the centre and pour over the mayonnaise mixed with the tomato ketchup and Worcester sauce. Serve with brown bread and butter and wedges of lemon.

Boiled Fresh Dublin Bay Prawns

8–12 Dublin Bay prawns, depending on size
1 carrot
1 small onion

1·25 litres (2½ pints) water
1 sprig parsley
Salt and 6 peppercorns
1 lemon
Mayonnaise

Peel and slice the carrot. Peel and slice the onion. Boil the carrot and onion in 1·25 litres (2½ pints) salted water for 10 minutes. Add the prawns, parsley, and peppercorns to the boiling water, and boil for 10–12 minutes. Leave the prawns to cool in the liquid. Remove the prawns and arrange them on a shallow serving dish. Garnish them with wedges of lemon and serve with mayonnaise.

Scampi Provençale

300 g (¾ lb.) frozen scampi
3 tablespoons olive oil
1 thinly sliced onion
1 clove garlic
3 ripe tomatoes
1 tablespoon finely chopped parsley
2 teaspoons lemon juice
Salt and freshly ground black pepper

Defrost the scampi and drain them well. Heat the oil and fry the onion and crushed garlic until transparent. Skin and slice the tomatoes and add to the onions with the scampi. Cook over a medium heat for 5–8 minutes until the scampi are just tender. Add the parsley and lemon juice and season well with salt and pepper. Serve on a bed of rice or by itself with hot French bread and butter.

SHRIMPS

Potted shrimps can be bought from most delicatessen stores. To make them go further one can add a carton of potted shrimps to 100 g (4 oz.) of melted butter seasoned with salt, freshly ground black pepper, a little juice and a pinch of mace.

Pour the melted mixture into a mould and leave to set. Turn out and decorate with a sprig of parsley. Serve with quarters of lemon and hot toast.

Fresh shrimps can be bought from most fishmongers, but, being so small they are devils to peel and I much prefer to buy prawns. Shrimps can be used for all prawn recipes.

CHAPTER EIGHT

MEAT

There are not many dishes made from a basis of meat that are suitable to serve as a first course and one has to be careful about balancing those there are with the course to follow – obviously barbecued spare-ribs followed by roast beef would make a most unsatisfactory meal.

Most pâtés in this section are rich and filling and should only be followed by a light dish. Many of them can be served as a main course for lunch or supper especially in the summer when they can be served with an attractive mixed salad and a few tiny new potatoes. My brisket of beef salad, which I love, could easily lure one into serving a badly balanced meal. Really it can only be followed by some form of fish, preferably one in a cream sauce, to provide a complete contrast to the texture of the beef.

The ham mousse is a useful recipe; so often one has some remains from a boiled or baked ham that are not enough to serve by themselves. Its lightness and piquancy lends itself well to a wide range of poultry and meat dishes to follow. Remains of roast or boiled meat, cut into thin matchstick strips, can be used in a variety of different sauces to serve as one of a selection of hors d'oeuvres.

ANTIPASTO OF COLD MEATS

In Italy it is usual to start a meal with an attractively arranged plate of cold thinly sliced sausages and meats of various kinds. Many of these meats are now available from good delicatessen shops in this country. Ask to have the sausages or meat sliced in the shop. Make sure that the silver paper covering is removed from salamis before they are cut; many shop-keepers have an aggravating habit of leaving it on and it takes ages to remove it from the meat once cut.

Allow 50 g (2 oz.) thinly sliced meat per serving. Remove any rinds or skins. Arrange 4–6 different varieties on individual plates. Garnish with black olives and/or radishes. Serve with French bread or rolls and butter.

VARIETIES OF MEATS TO SERVE AS ANTIPASTO
1. Bresaola – dried salt beef
2. Cacciatori – small salami
3. Coppa – salted pork
4. French garlic sausage
5. Mortadella – a pretty, pink, very large pork sausage dotted with small squares of white fat
6. Parma ham – smoked raw ham
7. Salami – the Milan variety is vastly superior to any other

PARMA HAM

A very delicately smoked raw ham from Italy. Most delicatessen stores sell it in tins. Some of the larger shops have the fresh product and will slice it for you.

Allow 50 g (2 oz.) ham per serving and arrange on individual plates. Serve thin slices of buttered brown bread separately.

Parma Ham and Melon

1 small honeydew melon
200 g (8 oz.) Parma ham

Cut the melon into 4 sections. Using a sharp knife cut between the flesh and the rind and, without disturbing the shape, cut it into bite sized pieces. Arrange thin slices of Parma ham over the top of the melon. Serve well chilled.

SMOKED MEAT AND POULTRY

Ham, beef, goose, turkey and chicken are now available in a
smoked form from many good delicatessen stores. Serve the
meat cut into wafer thin slices, arranged on a flat dish or on
individual plates. Garnish with crisp lettuce leaves and/or
tomatoes cut into quarters. Accompany smoked meat with a
horseradish sauce (see page 219) or Cumberland sauce.

Allow 50–75 g (2–3 oz.) per serving.

Springtime Beef Salad

1 medium cucumber
300 g ($\frac{3}{4}$ lb.) roast beef
125 ml ($\frac{1}{4}$ pint) double cream
2 teaspoons lemon juice
Salt, pepper and paprika
Crisp lettuce leaves
1 tablespoon chopped chives

Peel the cucumber and cut it into two lengthwise. Scoop out
the seeds and sprinkle the flesh with salt. Leave to drain for
1 hour and dry well on kitchen paper. Cut the flesh into very
small dice. Cut the beef into small dice. Whip the cream, mix
in the lemon juice and season with salt, pepper and paprika.
Fold the cucumber and meat into the cream. Arrange the
lettuce leaves on four plates. Arrange the salad on the lettuce
and sprinkle over the chopped chives.

Chill well before serving.

Brisket or Beef Salad

I seldom bother to make brisket of beef myself. It takes a long
time and a good grocer or delicatessen shop sells the meat,
evenly sliced, for a very reasonable price.

100 g ($\frac{1}{4}$ lb.) brisket (ask the grocer to cut it in very thin
slices – it goes further)

1 tablespoon sweet pickle
1 tablespoon horseradish sauce
125 ml ($\frac{1}{4}$ pint) double cream
Salt and pepper
Lettuce leaves
6 black olives

Cut the brisket into thin strips. Chop the sweet pickle finely. Mix the sweet pickle and horseradish sauce with the cream and season with salt and pepper. Fold the brisket into the cream sauce. Arrange in a shallow serving dish or on 4 small dishes, on a bed of lettuce leaves. Stone and chop the black olives and sprinkle them over the surface of the beef salad. Chill before serving.

Mortadella Salad

8 slices mortadella sausage
3 tablespoons olive oil
1 tablespoon wine vinegar
Salt and pepper

Remove the skin from the mortadella and cut the sausage into thin matchstick strips about 2·5 cm (1 inch) long. Combine the oil and vinegar and season with salt and pepper. Pour the dressing over the sausage and mix well. Arrange in a serving dish. Chill before serving.

Chinese Barbecued Spare-Ribs

Spare-ribs are very filling. They should only be served before a light main course but are so tasty and tantalizing that I could not resist including them in this book.

1 kg (2$\frac{1}{2}$ lbs.) lean spare-ribs of pork
25 g (1 oz.) sugar
3 tablespoons honey
4 tablespoons cider vinegar
3 tablespoons soy sauce

250 ml ($\frac{1}{2}$ pint) beef stock or consommé
2 minced garlic cloves
1 teaspoon powdered ginger

Trim off any fat from the spare-ribs. Cut them into individual ribs. Mix together the sugar, honey, vinegar, soy sauce, stock or consommé, garlic and ginger. Pour the sauce over the ribs and leave them to marinade for 2–3 hours, turning frequently. Arrange the ribs on a rack over a pan. Pour over the sauce. Bake in a medium oven (190 C., 375 F., Reg. 5) for 45–60 minutes, basting frequently with the juice.
Serve hot with the sauce poured over.

Frogs' Legs (Grenouilles)

Tinned frogs' legs are expensive and not very good, but it is now possible to buy frozen ones and they are excellent. The taste and texture of the legs are somewhat like those of very tender spring chicken. The meat is very easily digested. 3 pairs of frogs' legs should be prepared for each serving. If you are considering catching and preparing your own frogs, hunt for the large green ones. Having caught them and killed them humanely, remove the skin and cut off the legs above the thigh. Cut off the feet and soak the legs for six hours in salted water, changing the water three times.

Ham Croquettes

100 g (4 oz.) minced ham
125 g (5 oz.) fresh white breadcrumbs
25 g (1 oz.) grated cheese
$\frac{1}{2}$ teaspoon mixed herbs
1 tablespoon chopped onion
1 teaspoon dry mustard
1 large egg
Salt and pepper
Flour

1 egg white
Dry breadcrumbs
50 g (2 oz.) lard
Tomato sauce (see page 220)

Combine the ham, breadcrumbs, cheese, herbs, onion and dry mustard. Bind with the beaten egg and season with salt and pepper. If the mixture is too dry add a little milk. Form the mixture into sausage shapes. Roll them in flour, dip them in egg white and coat them with breadcrumbs. Fry the croquettes in hot lard until they are golden brown and crisp. Drain them on kitchen paper and serve hot with a tomato sauce.

Ham Rolls with Mushroom Sauce

200 g ($\frac{1}{2}$ lb.) button mushrooms
50 g (2 oz.) butter
250 ml ($\frac{1}{2}$ pint) cream
Salt and pepper
8 thin slices ham

Wash and dry the mushrooms. Slice them thinly and fry them lightly in half the butter for 5 minutes over a medium flame. Add the cream and season with salt and pepper. Keep warm but do not allow to boil. Melt the remaining butter in a frying pan. Fry the ham slices over a low flame for 1 minute only. Place some of the mushroom mixture on each slice of ham and roll up neatly. Place on a warm serving dish and serve immediately.

PÂTÉS AND TERRINES

PÂTÉ DE FOIE GRAS. The emperor of pâtés is the pâté de foie gras from Strasbourg, made from the pounded livers of fat geese flavoured with truffles. It is sold in attractive terrines which look as if they hold more than they in fact do, and retail at a very high price. The pâté is also sold in oblong tins for slightly less.

Pâté de foie gras should be served lightly chilled, straight from the terrine or cut into thin slices from the tin. It should be accompanied by fresh, hot toast and butter. Since it is extremely rich only a small quantity is required for each serving.

OTHER PÂTÉS. Basically most pâtés or terrines are made by combining a farce (mixture of pork sausage meat and other minced meat) with thin strips of meat, poultry, liver or game. The mixture is packed into a terrine lined with rashers of bacon and is baked in the oven. It is then left to cool and set. Smoother pâtés are made by finely mincing, grinding or blending all the ingredients before cooking them. They can be cooked in a pastry case or can be re-formed in a casing of aspic jelly. The use of herbs and flavourings is important in the making of all pâtés, since they give them the savoury taste that is essential.

Serve all pâtés with hot toast and butter.

Chicken Liver Pâté

200 g (8 oz.) chicken livers
1 onion
1 clove garlic
75 g (3 oz.) butter
1 tablespoon chopped parsley
$\frac{1}{4}$ teaspoon chopped thyme
$\frac{1}{4}$ teaspoon chopped savory
1 tablespoon brandy
Salt and freshly ground black pepper

Trim off any fat or fibres from the livers. Peel and finely chop the onion. Press the garlic through a garlic press. Melt 25 g (1 oz.) butter in a frying pan. Add the onion and garlic. Cook for 5 minutes over a medium flame until the onion is transparent and soft. Add the chicken livers and the herbs and cook for 3 minutes. Leave to cool and chop the livers. Melt the remaining butter and add it to the onion and livers. Pound in a pestle and mortar until the mixture is smooth (this can be done in an electric blender). Add the brandy and season well with salt and pepper. Pack the mixture into a lightly oiled mould and chill until set. Turn out the pâté and serve it with hot toast and butter.

Liver Sausage Pâté

> 200 g (8 oz.) liver sausage
> 50 g (2 oz.) butter
> ¼ teaspoon chopped parsley, chives, or marjoram (the herbs must be fresh)
> Salt and freshly ground black pepper
> A pinch of mace
> A pinch of nutmeg
> 1 clove garlic
> 2 teaspoons sherry or brandy

Skin the liver sausage and pound it with the butter. Mix in the chopped herbs and season with salt, pepper, mace, and nutmeg. Crush the garlic in a pestle and mortar or through a garlic press. Add the garlic and the sherry to the pâté and mix well. Press the pâté into a dish or small terrine and leave in a cool place to set. Serve with hot toast or French bread and butter.

Swedish Liver Pâté

This is a smooth creamy pâté. The meat, onions, and cream can be puréed in an electric blender in small quantities at a time.

> 200 g (½ lb.) calf liver
> 100 g (¼ lb.) pork fat
> 1 small onion
> 1 large or 2 small eggs
> 3 tablespoons double cream
> 1½ tablespoons flour
> 1½ tablespoons dry vermouth
> 50 g (2 oz.) button mushrooms (fresh or tinned)
> Salt and freshly ground black pepper

A pinch of ground ginger
A pinch of dried marjoram leaves
25 g (1 oz.) butter
Dill-pickled cucumber

Wash the liver and remove all the membranes. Cut the liver and pork into small pieces and grind it 5 times with the onions through a medium mincer. Add the eggs and beat well. Mix in the cream, flour, and vermouth. Slice the mushrooms and mix them with the meat. Season with salt, pepper, ginger, and marjoram. Stir until everything is very well mixed. Butter a small bread loaf pan thoroughly and spoon in the mixture. Cover with aluminium foil and bake in a pan filled with hot water in a very moderate oven (170 C., 325 F., Reg. 3) for $1\frac{1}{4}$ hours or until a knife inserted in the pâté comes out clean. Leave to cool in the pan. To serve, turn the pâté onto a serving dish, cut into slices and garnish with thin slices of dill-pickled cucumber.

Serve with hot toast and butter.

POTTED MEAT AND POULTRY
Nearly all meats, poultry and game are delicious potted with butter and spices. They make cheap and easy first courses and will keep for a considerable time if they are well sealed with clarified butter.

Potted Pigeon, Grouse or Partridge

At the right time of the year pigeons are really cheap and this recipe makes an ideal hors d'oeuvre for 4 servings or a luncheon dish for two. The carcasses can be used for making stock after the flesh has been removed.

2 plump pigeons or 1 grouse or partridge
8 juniper berries
A pinch of mace and cinnamon
150 g (6 oz.) butter
Salt and freshly ground black pepper

1 tablespoon brandy
4 rashers of bacon

Pound the juniper berries in a pestle and mortar with the mace, cinnamon, salt and pepper. When they are the size of coarsely ground pepper add 100 g (4 oz.) butter and mix well. Put a spoonful of the butter mixture inside each of the birds and rub the rest over the outside. Place them in a small casserole with the bacon. Pour over the brandy, cover tightly and bake in a cool oven (150 C., 300 F., Reg. 2) for 2 hours.

Drain off the cooking liquor from the birds and leave it to cool. Remove all the tender flesh and chop it into very small dice. Mix it with the bacon also cut into small dice. Pack the meat and bacon into an earthenware jar or terrine. Skim off the butter from the cooking liquor, melt it in a saucepan and pour it over the meat. Heat the remaining 50 g (2 oz.) butter until foaming and pour it over. It should completely cover the meat. If necessary add more butter. Leave to set in a cool place or a refrigerator. Serve cold with hot toast and butter.

Note: If properly sealed with clarified butter, potted game can be left for up to three weeks in a refrigerator.

CHAPTER NINE

VEGETABLES & FRUIT

Meat, fish and poultry are all becoming so expensive that we will all have to use vegetables as a main rather than a secondary ingredient. Where first courses are concerned the role of vegetables is a particularly valuable one; with imagination it is possible to produce the most exciting and delicious dishes from the most humble ingredients.

Artichauts à La Vinaigrette

4 large globe artichokes
French dressing

Trim off the stems of the artichokes and remove any tough outer leaves. With a pair of scissors cut off the top of the leaves so that you get a flat surface across the top. (This is not necessary but gives a professional touch.)

Plunge the artichokes, base down, into boiling salted water. Simmer for 30–40 minutes until tender. Test with a sharp knife to see if the heart is tender. Drain and leave to cool. Serve cold, with the French dressing passed round separately.

Note: Napkins and finger bowls are necessary.

Globe Artichokes Roman Style

It is difficult to buy artichokes small enough to cook in this manner since selling plants of giant proportions on the point of bursting into flower seems to be some kind of status symbol. When artichokes are eaten in this way every morsel, leaves, heart, and choke, are consumed so the plant must be exceptionally young and tender. If you grow your own, pick them before they grow to 5 cm (2 in.) in diameter.

2–3 small artichokes per serving
2 cloves garlic
Salt and pepper
Deep olive oil for frying

Trim off the stems and wash the artichokes in salted water. Leave them to drain, bottoms up, and when they are quite dry, trim off the points of the leaves with a pair of scissors. Chop the garlic very finely and insert it between the leaves of the artichokes. Sprinkle them with salt and pepper.

Heat the oil to smoking point and deep fry the artichokes for 10–15 minutes – the tips of the leaves should be crisply brown and the plant tender throughout. Drain them on a slotted spoon to remove all excess oil and flatten them gently to spread the leaves and to give the appearance of flower heads. Serve hot with melted butter.

ASPARAGUS

There are two main kinds of asparagus, the thinner green kind and the fat white stalks with just a little green at the tips. Since asparagus is difficult to establish and grow, it is unfortunately in the luxury price bracket.

Asparagus freezes well and although the frozen product is not quite as perfect as the fresh it is adequate. Tinned asparagus is not good enough to serve on its own as a first course, but makes a useful dish in a selection of hors d'oeuvres, served cold in a French dressing.

Asparagus as a first course is usually served hot with melted butter or sauce hollandaise, or cold with French dressing. Either way it is eaten in the fingers, held by the stalk which is then discarded.

Asparagus with Melted Butter

800 g (2 lbs.) asparagus
100g (4 oz.) butter

Cut off the tough white skin from the lower end of the stalks, trim them to uniform lengths and wash well. Tie the asparagus in 4 bundles and stand them, tips upwards, in a large pan of boiling salted water. Cook for 15–30 minutes, depending on the size of the stalks. Be careful not to overcook as the tips may drop off.

Drain carefully and untie the bundles. Arrange the asparagus on a warm flat serving dish and hand round hot melted butter separately.

Asparagus with Hollandaise Sauce

Cook the asparagus as above and serve with hollandaise sauce handed separately (see page 214).

Tinned Asparagus with Ham and Cheese

1 large tin of asparagus spears
8 thin slices ham
25 g (1 oz.) butter
25 g (1 oz.) flour
250 ml ($\frac{1}{2}$ pint) milk
Salt and pepper
75 g (3 oz.) grated Gruyère or Cheddar cheese

Drain the asparagus and divide into 8 portions. Wrap it in the ham and roll up neatly. Arrange the rolls in a serving dish.

Melt the butter in a saucepan, add the flour and mix well over a medium heat, gradually mix in the milk, stirring continually, and cook until the sauce is thick and smooth. Stir in half the cheese and season with salt and pepper. Pour the cheese sauce over the ham rolls and sprinkle the remaining cheese over the surface. Brown under a hot grill or in a hot oven. Serve hot.

Hot Stuffed Savoury Aubergine

4 small aubergines
3 tomatoes
1 green pepper

1 large onion
2 cloves garlic
2 tablespoons olive oil
100 g (4 oz.) boiled rice
1 tablespoon chopped parsley
Salt and pepper
50 g (2 oz.) grated cheese
4 anchovy fillets

Cut each aubergine in half lengthways. Cut lightly round the edge of the flesh and score several times across each half. Sprinkle with salt and leave to drain for ½ hour. Dry well and cook until soft, flat side down, in a little olive oil. Scoop out the flesh and chop finely. Arrange the skins in a shallow fire-proof dish.

Skin the tomatoes, remove the seeds and the core and chop the flesh finely. Seed and core the pepper and chop finely. Chop the onion and finely chop or mince the garlic. Heat the olive oil in a pan and add the onion, garlic, and green pepper. Cook over a medium heat for 15 minutes. Add the tomatoes, auberine flesh and boiled rice. Mix in the parsley and season with salt and pepper. Cover and cook for a further 15 minutes.

Fill the aubergine skins with the mixture and sprinkle with grated cheese. Arrange half an anchovy fillet on each half aubergine and bake for 10 minutes in a hot oven (220 C., 425 F., Reg. 7).

Aubergine Antipasto

4 large aubergines
6 tablespoons olive oil
600 g (1½ lb.) tomatoes
2 celery stalks
12 black olives
2 tablespoons capers
1 tablespoon lemon juice or wine vinegar
1 teaspoon sugar
Salt and freshly ground black pepper
1 tin anchovy fillets

Peel the aubergines and cut them into small dice. Sprinkle with salt and leave to sweat in a colander for half an hour. Dry the aubergines with kitchen paper or a clean cloth. Heat half the oil in a frying pan. Add the aubergines and cook over a fast flame until browned on all sides. Remove from the heat. Peel the tomatoes and cut into dice. Thinly slice the celery. Pit and slice the olives. Heat the remaining oil in a saucepan. Add the tomatoes and celery and cook over a low heat for 10 minutes. Add the olives, drained capers, lemon juice (or vinegar) and sugar. Season with salt and pepper. Simmer for 20 minutes until the celery is quite tender. Stir in the aubergines and cook for a further 10 minutes stirring well. Check seasoning and leave to cool. Arrange the aubergine mixture in a shallow serving dish and decorate with the drained anchovy fillets. Heat if desired, in a fairly hot oven (200 C., 400 F., Reg. 6) for 10 minutes. This antipasto can be served hot or chilled. I prefer it chilled served with hot toast and butter. This makes a perfect filling for rich pastry tartlets (see page 178).

Avocado Pears with Prawns and Onions

2 ripe avocados
100 g (4 oz.) peeled prawns
1 small jar cocktail onions
2 tablespoons olive oil
$\frac{2}{3}$ tablespoon white wine vinegar
Salt and freshly ground black pepper

Cut the avocados in half and remove the stone. Drain the onions and divide the prawns and onions between the four halves of pears, filling the central cavities. Combine the olive oil and vinegar. Mix well and season with salt and pepper. Pour the dressing over the pears. Chill well before serving.

Avocado Pears with Orange and Watercress

2 small ripe avocados
1 orange
1 bunch of watercress, chopped
1 teaspoon Dijon mustard
3 tablespoons olive oil
1 tablespoon white wine vinegar
Salt and pepper

Peel the avocados and cut them in half. Remove the stones and slice thinly. Peel the orange and remove any white membrane. Cut the orange into thin slices and arrange in a dish with the avocado slices and the chopped watercress. Add a little of the olive oil to the mustard and mix well. Stir in the rest of the olive oil. Add the vinegar, season well with salt and pepper and mix well before pouring over the avocados, orange and watercress. Chill before serving.

Avocado Pear Mould

A versatile mould which you can serve with a variety of different fillings. A good dish for a buffet party.

2 avocados (make sure they are not bruised)
2 tablespoons water
2 teaspoons lemon juice
15 g ($\frac{1}{2}$ oz.) gelatine
125 ml ($\frac{1}{4}$ pint) chicken stock, made with a cube
1 teaspoon grated onion
2 teaspoons Worcester sauce
125 ml ($\frac{1}{4}$ pint) double cream
125 ml ($\frac{1}{4}$ pint) mayonnaise
Salt and freshly ground black pepper

Melt the gelatine in the water and lemon juice over a gentle heat. Add the chicken stock and leave to cool. Peel the avocados and remove the stones. Mash the flesh with the grated onion and Worcester sauce. Stir in the gelatine mixture and mix well until it has melted. Leave until almost set. Whip the cream until fairly stiff. Fold the mayonnaise and the cream into the avocado mixture. Season with salt and pepper.

Damp a ring mould with cold water. Spoon in the mixture and leave in a refrigerator to set. Turn out the mould and serve chilled with one of the following mixtures or anything else that you fancy.

1. 100 g (4 oz.) prawns
   2 tablespoons chopped green pepper
   French dressing

Combine the ingredients and arrange in the centre of the mould.

2. 2 tomatoes
   1 small tin tuna fish
   1 tablespoon chopped chives
   French dressing

Peel and dice the tomatoes. Drain the tuna and flake the flesh with a fork. Mix the tomatoes, tuna and French dressing. Arrange in the centre of the mould. Sprinkle the chopped chives over.

3. 1 tin crab
   2 tablespoons chopped pimento
   1 tablespoon chopped chives or spring onions
   French dressing

Drain the crab, remove any hard filaments and flake. Combine the crab, pimento, chopped chives or spring onions and French dressing. Arrange in the centre of the mould.

Les Crudités

During a week spent in the South of France one year I ate crudités as a first course for lunch every single day, never tiring of the way the raw vegetable selections were arranged and scraping up the last drop of the strong garlic flavoured mayonnaise.

The ingredients for the crudités vary according to the season but the basis is always tender raw vegetables supplemented with hard boiled eggs, served in their shells, thin slices of salami or garlic sausage or thin slices of cheese. A lot of the joy of crudités lies in its arrangement. Arrange the vegetables in groups, on a long shallow dish, surrounding a bowl of garlic mayonnaise or aïoli.

This recipe is for a typical dish of crudités to serve in the early summer when vegetables are at their best. The dish is left in the centre of the table. Everyone helps themselves to the selection they want and dips each bit into the mayonnaise. Use fingers whenever possible.

3 carrots
6 spring onions
1 green pepper
1 bunch radishes
3 tender sticks celery
1 bunch watercress
$\frac{1}{2}$ small cucumber
4 hard boiled eggs
4 very small firm tomatoes
250 ml ($\frac{1}{2}$ pint) garlic mayonnaise or aïoli (see page 211)

Peel or scrape the carrots, trim them, and cut them lengthways into thin sticks. Clean and trim the onions leaving a good portion of green stalk. Core and seed the pepper and cut it into thin strips. Wash the radishes in iced water. Remove the tails but leave about 2·5 cm (1 in.) of the green top on each. Trim the celery and cut each piece in three lengthways. Trim off the tough stalks of the watercress. Cut the cucumber lengthways into 8 pieces. Arrange the vegetables attractively on a shallow dish with the whole unpeeled hard boiled eggs and whole tomatoes and place the bowl of mayonnaise in the centre. Serve with French or granary bread and with a dish of butter.

Cucumber Mould

A good basis for many exciting fillings – very cool and refreshing to look at.

1 large cucumber
15 g ($\frac{1}{2}$ oz.) gelatine
1 tablespoon sugar
250 ml ($\frac{1}{2}$ pint) water
Juice of 1 large lemon
2 tablespoons dry white wine
Salt

Peel and thinly slice the cucumber, and sprinkle the slices with a little salt. Combine the gelatine, sugar and water in a saucepan. Heat gently until the gelatine has melted. Add the lemon juice and white wine to the gelatine mixture and leave until cool. Pour a thin layer of the jelly into the bottom of a ring mould. Leave in a refrigerator until set. Place a layer of cucumber over the jelly, cover with more jelly and leave to set. Repeat the layers of cucumber and jelly until the mould is filled. Leave in a refrigerator to set.

Turn out the mould by dipping it in hot water for 1 second. Fill the centre with one of the following mixtures or any combination you have at hand. Serve chilled.

Fillings
 1. 1 avocado pear
    200 g ($\frac{1}{4}$ lb.) peeled prawns
    French dressing

Peel the avocado and remove the stone. Dice the flesh and mix it with the prawns and French dressing. Spoon the mixture into the centre of the ring mould.

 2. 200 g ($\frac{1}{2}$ lb.) cream cheese
    $\frac{1}{2}$ chopped green pepper
    1 tablespoon chopped red pimento
    6 chopped stuffed olives
    2 tablespoons chopped chives or spring onions
    Salt and pepper

Add the chopped green pepper, pimento, stuffed olives, and chives to the cream cheese. Mix well and season with salt and pepper. Spoon into the centre of the cucumber mould. Serve chilled.

> 3. 1 bunch watercress
> 1 avocado pear
> French dressing

Chop the watercress leaves. Peel the avocado and remove the stone. Dice the flesh. Combine the watercress, avocado and French dressing. Spoon into the centre of the cucumber mould. Serve chilled.

MELON

There is a great difference between a tasteless slice of under-ripe melon and one that is served in prime condition. Melons are divided into three varieties, Cantaloup, Honeydew and Charentais, of which the small Charentais is vastly the best. The flesh is soft and full of flavour. The Honeydew is much crisper and needs to be fully ripened before serving. The Cantaloup is, I think, rather tasteless and often has a slightly woolly texture. Test melons for ripeness by gently pushing the skin at the end opposite the stalk. It should give slightly but not be squashy.

Melons should be served chilled and since they have a very pervading smell it is wise to keep them wrapped in a polythene bag in the refrigerator.

Melon with Prawns

> 100 g (4 oz.) peeled prawns
> $\frac{1}{2}$ Honeydew melon
> 125 ml ($\frac{1}{4}$ pint) mayonnaise
> Paprika pepper
> 1 lettuce

Peel the melon and remove the seeds. Cut the melon into small cubes or into balls with a vegetable scoop. Combine the melon and the prawns with half the mayonnaise. Season with a little paprika pepper. Shred the lettuce and arrange it at the bottom of four glass dishes. Spoon over the melon and prawns and cover with the remainder of the mayonnaise. Serve chilled.

Melon with Blackcurrants

2 small Charentais melons
1 medium tin of blackcurrants
2 teaspoons lemon juice

Choose ripe melons. Cut each melon in half and remove the seeds. Scoop out the flesh and cut it into small cubes. In a bowl combine the melon with the blackcurrants and the lemon juice. Mix gently and spoon into the melon shells. Serve the melon in individual glass bowls on a bed of crushed ice.

Simone's Orange and Watercress Salad

An inexpensive dish with a subtle flavour.

3 oranges
2 bunches of watercress
3 tablespoons olive oil
1 tablespoon vinegar
1 teaspoon curry paste or powder
Salt and pepper

Peel the oranges and divide them into segments. Remove all the skin, pips, and membrane from the segments. Cut off any tough stems from the watercress and roughly chop the leaves. Combine the oil, vinegar, and curry paste or powder. Season with salt and pepper and mix well. Pour the dressing over the oranges and watercress and toss gently together. Chill before serving.

Pears Roquefort

2 large eating pears
100 g (4 oz.) Roquefort cheese (or blue cheese)
125 ml ($\frac{1}{4}$ pint) mayonnaise
Lettuce leaves

Peel the pears and cut each one in half. Scoop out the core and fill the holes with cheese. Arrange each filled half-pear on lettuce leaves and pour over the mayonnaise. Serve chilled.

Note: I am not a great advocate for combinations of fruit and mayonnaise but this is an exception. It is a particularly good dish to serve on a hot summer evening.

Peperonata

A classic Italian vegetable starter, made two days in advance.

400 g (1 lb.) green peppers
4 ripe tomatoes
2 Spanish onions
3 tablespoons olive oil
4 tablespoons white wine vinegar
Salt and freshly ground black pepper
A screw top jar

Seed and core the peppers. Cut them into thin strips. Peel and dice the tomatoes. Peel and thinly slice the onions. Put the peppers, tomatoes and onions into a saucepan with the olive oil. Heat, cover and simmer for one hour. Stir occasionally to prevent sticking. Add the vinegar and season with salt and pepper. Continue to cook uncovered for a further 20 minutes. Cool and put into a screw top jar. Leave in a refrigerator for 2 days before serving. Serve chilled.

Note: Chopped anchovies or olives can be added before serving.

Primavera Salad

800 g (2 lbs.) young broad beans
100 g (¼ lb.) thinly sliced ham
1 green pepper
1 teaspoon Dijon mustard
3 tablespoons olive oil
1 tablespoon white wine vinegar
Salt and pepper
Chervil or parsley

Shell the beans and cook them in boiling salted water for 10–15 minutes until they are just tender. Leave to cool. Seed and core the green pepper and cut it into very thin matchstick strips. Cut the ham into very thin strips.

Combine the mustard, olive oil, vinegar, and seasoning and mix well. Pour the dressing over the beans, pepper, and ham and toss them together. Sprinkle the surface with finely chopped chervil if you have it – if not parsley will do. Serve chilled with hot French bread or with cheese straws.

Ratatouille

Although ratatouille is often served as a vegetable dish with a main course, it is a very good starter to any meal. Which vegetables you use really depends on availability and individual taste but aubergines, onions, and tomatoes are essential. The courgettes can be replaced by marrow or cucumber, or left out entirely. Tinned tomatoes can be used instead of fresh ones.

3 medium aubergines
2 cloves garlic
2 courgettes (Italian marrows)
2 large onions
2 green or red peppers
4 large ripe tomatoes
Salt and freshly ground black pepper
1 teaspoon basil
4 tablespoons olive oil

Chop the aubergines and the courgettes into small dice, leaving the skin on. Put them into a colander, well sprinkled with salt, and leave them to sweat for $\frac{1}{2}$ hour.

Finely chop the garlic and cut the onions into very thin slices. Seed and chop the peppers and chop the tomatoes. Heat the olive oil and add the onion. Cook until the onion is transparent over a medium heat. Add the garlic and cook for a further 5 minutes; do not allow the onion to brown. Dry the aubergine and courgette. Add them to the onion with the chopped peppers. Cover and cook for 30 minutes over a low flame. Add the tomatoes and the basil. Season well with salt and pepper. Cover and continue to cook over a low flame for a further 30 minutes. Drain off any excess oil.

Hot Ratatouille

Sprinkle 50 g (2 oz.) grated Parmesan cheese over the ratatouille and brown under a hot grill before serving.

Chilled Ratatouille

Chill the ratatouille and sprinkle with chopped parsley before serving.

Salade Niçoise

    2 lettuce hearts
    1 tin tuna fish
    8 stoned black olives
    1 hard boiled egg
    1 small tin anchovy fillets
    2 tomatoes
    100 g ($\frac{1}{4}$ lb.) cooked French beans (or 1 small tin French beans)
    $\frac{1}{2}$ chopped red pepper
DRESSING
    1 clove garlic
    1 teaspoon Dijon mustard

3 tablespoons olive oil
1 tablespoon white wine vinegar
Salt and pepper
1 teaspoon chervil

Cut the lettuce hearts into quarters and arrange them in a salad bowl. Drain the tuna fish and break it into pieces with a fork. Arrange the tuna fish in the centre of the lettuce. Decorate with the egg, cut into quarters, the stoned olives, the anchovies, the quartered tomatoes, the chopped green beans, and the red pepper.

Crush the garlic and mix it well with the mustard. Gradually mix in the olive oil. Add the vinegar, season with salt and pepper. Add the chopped chervil and mix well. Pour the dressing over the salad and serve chilled with hot French bread or rolls.

TOMATOES

Locally grown tomatoes ripened on the plant are infinitely preferable to those imported or ripened by artificial means, and it is these firm sweet fruits that should be used for stuffing and serving as a cold hors d'oeuvre. Imported tomatoes are useful for salads, flavouring, decoration and garnish. Tinned tomatoes can be used instead of fresh ones in dishes that are to be served hot and where it is the tomato flavour and not the appearance which is important. Use the tiny cherry tomatoes whole in salads and for decoration.

Always wash tomatoes in cold running water before serving them. The fruit and plants are so often sprayed with strong manures and fertilizers that a trace of an unpleasant tasting substance may easily remain.

TO PEEL TOMATOES. Pour boiling water over washed tomatoes and leave it for a few seconds only. Prick the skins with a sharp knife and the skin will slide easily off the flesh.

Tomatoes Stuffed with Cucumber

8 medium tomatoes
1 cucumber
1 tablespoon chopped chives
250 ml ($\frac{1}{2}$ pint) double cream
Salt, pepper and paprika
Watercress for garnish

Cut a slice off the tops of the tomatoes. Using a spoon scoop out the insides of the tomatoes taking care not to pierce the skins. Discard the seeds and core and roughly chop the flesh. Peel the cucumber and cut it in half lengthwise. Remove the seeds and cut the flesh into small dice. Sprinkle with salt and leave to drain in a colander for $\frac{1}{2}$ hour.

Whip the cream lightly. Fold in the tomato, chives, and cucumber, and season with salt, pepper, and paprika. Stuff the mixture into the tomato shells and chill well before serving. Garnish with watercress.

Hot Savoury Stuffed Tomatoes

4 large tomatoes
200 g (8 oz.) mushrooms
1 medium onion
3 rashers of bacon
3 tablespoons olive oil
1 tablespoon finely chopped parsley
1 teaspoon chopped basil and chervil
Salt and pepper
1 beaten egg
2 tablespoons fine breadcrumbs
50 g (2 oz.) butter

Cut the tomatoes in half. Scoop out the insides with a spoon taking care not to pierce the skin. Discard the seeds and core and chop the flesh. Wash the mushrooms and chop them. Chop the onion and the bacon. Heat the oil in a pan. Add the mushrooms, onion, bacon, parsley, chopped tomatoes, and herbs. Cook over a medium heat for 10 minutes. Stir in the beaten egg and season with salt and pepper.

Fill the tomatoes with the mixture and arrange them on a shallow fireproof dish. Sprinkle over the breadcrumbs and dot with the butter. Bake for 30 minutes in a fairly hot oven (200 C., 400 F., Reg. 6). Serve hot.

Tomatoes Stuffed with Cream Cheese

8 medium tomatoes
200 g ($\frac{1}{2}$ lb.) cream cheese
2 teaspoons chopped parsley
2 teaspoons chopped chives
50 g (2 oz.) chopped ham
Salt, pepper and paprika
Watercress

Wash the tomatoes and remove the stalks. Cut a wide slice off the top of each one. Scoop out the inside with a teaspoon being careful not to break through the skin. Mix the cheese with the chopped chives, parsley and ham. Season with salt, pepper and a pinch of paprika. Fill the tomatoes with the cheese mixture and replace the caps. Serve chilled. Garnish with sprigs of watercress.

Stuffed Vine Leaves (Dolmades)

1 tin vine leaves
1 tablespoon olive oil
100 g (4oz.) minced new lamb
100g (4 oz.) rice
1 finely chopped medium onion
Salt and pepper
500 ml (1 pint) chicken stock
Juice of $\frac{1}{2}$ lemon
1 tablespoon chopped parsley
1 tablespoon tomato purée
1 tablespoon cream

Heat the oil in a saucepan. Add the minced meat, rice and chopped onion. Cook over a medium heat for 10 minutes. Season with salt and pepper. Pour over enough water to cover the rice and meat. Mix in the lemon juice and parsley. Cover and simmer for 20 minutes.

Spread out the vine leaves and put a spoonful of stuffing in the centre of each one. Roll up the leaves into neat parcels and arrange them in a baking dish. Pour over the stock and bake for 1 hour in a moderate oven (180 C., 350 F., Reg. 4).

Drain off the liquid and reheat with the cream and tomato purée. Pour the sauce over the vine leaves and serve hot.

CHAPTER TEN

PASTA, PASTRY & PANCAKES

PASTA

Personally, I think that most forms of pasta are far too heavy to serve as a first course, but there are a few recipes which I do use to precede a very light main course, or if I know that my guests are really great trenchermen. Canneloni, ravioli, gnocchi, and spaghetti served with a heavy meat sauce are *out*. Buy only the genuine Italian pasta. Imitation versions tend to be gluey and unappetizing.

Spaghetti Maratea

200 g (½ lb.) spaghetti
50 g (2 oz.) butter
2 rashers chopped bacon
1 tablespoon grated Parmesan cheese
1 tin asparagus tips
2 eggs
Salt and freshly ground black pepper

Plunge the unbroken spaghetti into a large saucepan of fast boiling salt water. Cook for 20 minutes until just tender. (The only way to test spaghetti is to dig out a bit and chew it.) Drain well. Melt the butter in a large frying pan. Fry the chopped bacon in the butter for 3–5 minutes until soft but not browned. Add the spaghetti, cheese, drained asparagus tips and the lightly beaten eggs. Cook over a low heat, stirring gently with a fork, until it is hot through and the eggs are just beginning to set. Season with salt and pepper and serve immediately.

Liza's Tagliatelle Verdi

Liza was a cook in a house where I used to stay as a child.

200 g ($\frac{1}{2}$ lb.) tagliatelle verdi (flat spaghetti flavoured with spinach and green in colour)
200 g ($\frac{1}{2}$ lb.) fresh or frozen peas
4 poached eggs
250 ml ($\frac{1}{2}$ pint) mayonnaise

Cook the tagliatelle verdi in plenty of just boiling salted water, for 20 minutes or until just tender. Drain well and leave to cool. Cook the peas in boiling salted water until tender. Drain and cool. Combine the tagliatelle and the peas and arrange them on a flat serving dish. Poach the eggs in boiling water (see page 197). Drain, cool and trim away untidy edges. Place the eggs on the bed of tagliatelle and peas and mask them with mayonnaise. Serve lightly chilled.

PASTRY

Many dishes made with pastry make good first courses. Best known are vol au vents filled with creamed meat, poultry or fish and the many quiches (filled pastry flans usually baked blind without the filling).

All pastry is easiest to manage when it is chilled. It is worth waiting an extra half an hour to ensure that it is really cold before rolling out. Trouble should be taken to roll out the pastry as thinly as possible: thick pastry may be a better shape but it is most unappetizing. Most pastry dishes can be served either cold or hot. Take care over reheating pastry as it will continue to cook and is liable to burn.

PUFF PASTRY

I am including a recipe for puff pastry but I must admit that I have only made it about half a dozen times in my life. Now that ready made commercial puff pastry is easy to buy, either fresh from a baker's shop, or frozen, I use the bought product and it really is very good indeed. Use fresh puff pastry the day it is bought and frozen puff pastry as soon as it has defrosted. Always chill the pastry before using it.

200 g (8 oz.) chilled butter
200 g (8 oz.) plain flour
Salt
125 ml ($\frac{1}{4}$ pint) iced water

Sieve the flour and salt into a bowl. Add 25 g (1 oz.) butter and rub it into the flour until the mixture resembles coarse bread-crumbs. Mix the paste to a firm dough with the water. Roll out the dough on a lightly floured board, to a rectangle 1 cm ($\frac{1}{2}$ inch) thick. Place the butter in a square slab in the centre of the pastry. Fold the sides of the pastry over so that the butter is completely covered. Press the edges together. Wrap the pastry in a cloth and chill for 20 minutes.

Place the chilled dough on a floured board with a pressed end towards you. Roll out the pastry to 1 cm ($\frac{1}{2}$ inch) thick being careful that the butter doesn't break out of the sides. Fold both ends of the pastry towards the centre. Give a half turn to the pastry and roll out once more. Fold and roll and fold again twice more.

Wrap the pastry in a cloth and chill it for a further 20 minutes before re-rolling and refolding as above, three times. Re-wrap and re-chill the pastry before re-rolling and re-folding for a final couple of times. Chill before finally rolling and using the pastry.

Vol Au Vents

Vol au vents are crisp light pastry cases made from puff pastry, baked without a filling. They can either be made as one large case or many smaller ones and can be filled with a variety of fish, shellfish and meat fillings in a sauce.

They can be re-heated or served at room temperature.

To Make Small Vol Au Vents
Puff pastry
Beaten egg

Roll out the pastry to $\frac{1}{2}$ cm ($\frac{1}{4}$ inch) thick. Cut into 4 cm ($1\frac{1}{2}$ inch) rounds with a fluted pastry cutter. Cut out the centres of *half* the rounds with a 2·5 cm (1 inch) cutter. Brush the pastry rings with water and press them carefully over the full circles. Dampen a baking sheet. Arrange the circles on the baking sheet. Replace the cut outs in the centres. Brush lightly with beaten egg and chill for 20 minutes. Bake the vol au vents in a hot oven (230 C., 450 F., Reg. 8) for 10 minutes. Reduce the heat to moderate (180 C., 350 F., Reg. 4) and continue to cook for a further 5 minutes. Leave to cool and carefully remove the cut-out centres. Fill with whatever mixture you are using, and replace the tops. Reheat in a moderate oven (180 C., 350 F., Reg. 4) or serve at room temperature.

To Make a Large Vol Au Vent Case
Puff pastry
Beaten egg

Roll out the pastry to 1 cm ($\frac{1}{2}$ inch) thick. Using a plate or saucepan lid about 23 cm (9 inches) in diameter, cut round the edge with a sharp knife, sloping the knife outwards to help the rise of the pastry. Reverse the pastry onto a wet baking sheet. Place a plate or saucepan lid, of a size that will leave a 5 cm (2 inch) border of pastry round the edge, in the centre of the pastry. Using a sharp knife cut half way through the pastry. Mark the border with a criss cross pattern. Brush the top with beaten egg taking care not to let it run down the side of the pastry. Bake the pastry case in a hot oven (230 C., 450 F., Reg. 8) for 20 minutes or until it has risen and is golden brown. Reduce the heat to moderate (180 C., 350 F., Reg. 4) and cook for a further 5 minutes.

Cut round the inner circle of the case and gently lift off the lid. Remove any soft pastry in the centre. Fill, replace the top, reheat in a moderate oven (180 C., 350 F., Reg. 4) or serve at room temperature.

Fillings for Vol Au Vents
1. *Seafood Filling*
    200 g ($\frac{1}{2}$ lb.) prawns
    100 g ($\frac{1}{4}$ lb.) lobster, crabmeat, or scampi
    40 g (1$\frac{1}{2}$ oz.) butter
    40 g (1$\frac{1}{2}$ oz.) flour
    125ml ($\frac{1}{4}$ pint) milk
    Salt, pepper, and a pinch of paprika pepper
    2 tablespoons cream
    1 tablespoon sherry

Chop the lobster or flake the crabmeat. Melt the butter in a saucepan. Add the flour and mix well. Gradually add the milk, stirring constantly over a medium heat until the sauce is thick and smooth. Add the prawns and lobster. Mix well and season with salt, pepper and pinch of paprika. Cook for 3 minutes. Stir in the cream and the sherry. Spoon the mixture into hot vol au vent cases or cool it before spooning it into cold cases and reheating in a medium oven (190 C., 375 F., Reg. 5) for 5 minutes until hot through.

2. *Chicken Filling*
    200 g ($\frac{1}{2}$ lb.) cooked chicken
    200 g ($\frac{1}{2}$ lb.) mushrooms
    50 g (2 oz.) butter
    40 g (1$\frac{1}{2}$ oz.) flour
    125 ml ($\frac{1}{4}$ pint) milk
    Salt and pepper
    2 tablespoons cream
    1 tablespoon chopped parsley

Cut the chicken into small pieces. Wash, dry, and chop the mushrooms. Melt 15 g ($\frac{1}{2}$ oz.) butter in a saucepan. Gently cook the mushrooms for 3 minutes. Set aside. Melt remaining butter in a saucepan. Add the flour and mix well. Gradually add in the milk, stirring constantly until the sauce is thick and smooth. Add the chicken and the mushrooms to the sauce. Season with salt and pepper and cook for a further 3

minutes. Add the cream and chopped parsley. Fill hot cases
with the hot chicken or cold cases with cooled chicken and
reheat in a medium oven (190 C., 375 F., Reg. 5) for 5 minutes
or until hot through.

QUICHES OR SAVOURY TARTS

The secret of most quiches is their simplicity. One or two
ingredients are used as the basis, and covered by a luxurious
savoury custard. The basic quiche pastry is easy to make;
success comes with the minimum amount of handling. Chill
the pastry well before rolling it as thinly as possible and lining
the flan tin. A thick pastry becomes tough, heavy and soggy
when cooked. Bake your quiche on a metal baking sheet –
then the bottom will be cooked through and crisp.

Basic Quiche or Savoury Tart Pastry

100 g (4 oz.) plain flour
Salt and pepper
50 g (2 oz.) butter
1 beaten egg
1 tablespoon iced water

Sieve the flour with some salt and pepper onto a wooden
board or marble slab. Make a well in the centre. Cut the butter
into small pieces and place it with the egg and water in the well.
Gradually mix the flour into the butter, egg and water using
the tips of the fingers. Form the pastry into a ball and chill it
for at least an hour before rolling it out. Roll out the pastry on
a floured board, very thinly, and line a 23 cm (9 inch) flan tin.

Mushroom Quiche

100 g (4 oz.) plain flour
Salt and pepper
50 g (2 oz.) butter
1 egg
1 tablespoon iced water
200 g (8 oz.) firm mushrooms

65 g (2½ oz.) butter
40 g (1½ oz.) flour
250 ml (½ pint) milk
Salt and pepper

Make the pastry as shown above.

Roll it out on a floured board, as thinly as possible and line a 23 cm (9 inch) flan tin. Prick the bottom of the flan with a fork. Place a circle of waxed paper over the pastry. Fill it with dried peas or beans or rice. Bake the pastry case in a medium oven (190 C., 375 F., Reg. 5) for 15–20 minutes until golden and crisp.Remove the paper and dried peas. Leave to cool.

Wash and dry the mushrooms. Cut them into thin slices through the caps and stalks. Melt 25 g (1 oz.) butter in a saucepan. Cook the mushrooms over a medium heat for 6 minutes. Melt 40 g (1½ oz.) butter in another saucepan. Add the flour and mix well. Gradually blend in the milk stirring continually over a medium heat until the sauce boils and is thick and smooth. Add the mushrooms and season with salt and pepper. Pour the mixture into the flan case. Heat through in a fairly hot oven (200 C., 400 F., Reg. 6) for 5–8 minutes. Serve hot.

Rich Pastry Tartlets or Barquettes

This pastry is very crisp. It is difficult to deal with but well worth the trouble and is especially suitable for serving with a cold filling. The secret of the pastry lies in chilling it really well.

200 g (½ lb.) plain flour
Salt
100 g (¼ lb.) butter
1 egg
2 hard boiled egg yolks

Sieve the flour and the salt onto a pastry board or marble slab. Make a well in the centre. Cut the butter into small pieces and place it with the egg in the well. Mash the egg yolks and add them to the butter and egg. Work the butter and eggs into a paste using the fingertips. Gradually draw in the flour and continue to blend with the fingertips until a smooth dough is formed. Wrap the pastry in a clean cloth and chill it in a refrigerator for a good two hours. Divide the chilled pastry into two portions. Roll each portion between two sheets of grease-proof paper until the pastry is almost thin enough to see through. Cut the pastry into 5 cm (2 inch) circles and line tartlet tins. Press the pastry against the side of the tins with the ball of the thumb. Chill the pastry again before baking. This should be done in the freezing compartment of the refrigerator for at least half an hour before baking. Prick the bottoms of the tartlets. Bake in a pre-heated medium oven (190 C., 375 F., Reg. 5) for 10 minutes until the tartlets are a pale golden brown. Cool in the tins and turn out carefully. Fill with the required filling.

Note: Unfilled tartlet cases can be kept for two or three days in an air-tight tin.

Fillings for Tartlets or Barquettes
1. Flaked tuna fish mixed with a little whipped cream and seasoned with lemon juice, salt, and pepper.
2. Smoked salmon spread.
3. Cream cheese, seasoned with salt and pepper and mixed with finely chopped chives.
4. Prawns mixed with a thick mayonnaise.
5. Prawns mixed with cream cheese and chopped chives.
6. Aubergine antipasto – See page 157.
7. Pâté.
8. Chicken livers and mushrooms finely chopped and well seasoned with salt and freshly ground black pepper, cooked in butter and cooled.
9. Caviar topped with a teaspoon of whipped soured cream.

Savoury Puffs

These are the savoury version of éclairs or cream puffs.

250 ml ($\frac{1}{2}$ pint) water
75 g (3 oz.) butter
$\frac{1}{4}$ teaspoon salt
125 g (5 oz.) plain flour
3 eggs
1 beaten egg
1 tablespoon milk

Put the water and the butter into a saucepan. Add the salt and bring to the boil. Boil until the butter has all melted. Remove from the heat. Add the flour all at once and beat it with a wooden spoon until the mixture forms a smooth ball and leaves the sides of the pan. Add the eggs one by one, beating each one in until the paste is smooth and shiny – about 2 minutes. Drop the pastry from a teaspoon onto a buttered baking dish. Brush with a mixture of beaten egg and milk. Bake for 15 minutes in a fairly hot oven (200 C., 400 F., Reg. 6) until the puffs are golden and dry. Open the oven door and leave them for a further 2 minutes. Leave the puffs to cool. Make an insertion with a sharp knife three quarters way up the puffs, leaving a hinged lid. Fill the puffs with a filling and reheat for a few minutes in a moderate oven (180 C., 350 F., Reg. 4) or serve at room temperature.

Note: The puffs can be filled in advance and reheated just before being served.

Fillings for Savoury Puffs
1. *Ham Filling*
   200 g (8 oz.) minced ham
   250 ml ($\frac{1}{4}$ pint) double cream
   Juice of $\frac{1}{2}$ lemon
   Salt, pepper, and a pinch of cayenne

Combine all the ingredients. Season with salt, pepper and a pinch of cayenne. Put a little of the mixture in each puff. Reheat in a moderate oven (180 C., 350 F., Reg. 4) for 5 minutes. Serve at once. A tomato sauce can be served with ham-filled puffs.

2. *Cheese Filling*
   25 g (1 oz.) butter
   25 g (1 oz.) flour
   250 ml (½ pint) milk
   50 g (2 oz.) grated Cheddar cheese
   Salt, pepper, and a pinch of paprika
   25 g (1 oz.) grated Parmesan cheese

Melt the butter in a saucepan. Add the flour and mix well. Gradually add the milk, stirring continually over a moderate heat until the sauce is thick and smooth. Add the Cheddar cheese. Season with salt, pepper, and a pinch of paprika. Continue to cook over a moderate heat for a further 3 minutes. Fill the puffs with the cheese sauce. Sprinkle them with the Parmesan cheese and reheat in a moderate oven (180 C., 350 F., Reg. 4) for 5–8 minutes. Serve at once.

3. *Sardine Filling*
   1 tin sardines
   125 ml (¼ pint) double cream
   Juice of half a lemon
   1 teaspoon chopped tarragon
   1 teaspoon chopped parsley
   Salt and pepper

Drain the sardines. Mash them with a fork and mix them with the cream. Add the lemon juice, tarragon and parsley. Season with salt and pepper and mix well until a smooth paste is formed. Fill the puffs with the sardine filling. Reheat in a moderate oven (180 C., 350 F., Reg. 4) for 5 minutes. Serve at once.

Note: Fillings recommended for pastry barquettes, vol au vents, and croustades may also be used but the ingredients must be finely chopped.

Croustades (Baked Bread Cases)

These make useful alternatives to barquettes or vol au vent cases.

1 loaf white bread
50 g (2 oz.) melted butter

Cut the bread into 2·5 cm (1 inch) slices. Trim off crusts and cut the slices into 4 squares. With a sharp-pointed knife cut out the centre of the squares to the depth of 18 mm ($\frac{3}{4}$ inch), leaving a 6 mm ($\frac{1}{4}$ inch) surround at the edge of the squares. Brush melted butter all over the sides and the top of the squares. Bake them in a hot oven (230 C., 450 F., Reg. 8) for 5 minutes or until crisp and golden brown. Cool and fill. Reheat in a medium oven (190 C., 375 F., Reg. 5) or serve at room temperature.

Allow 3 croustades per serving.

Fillings for Croustades

1. *Creamed Mushrooms*

300 g (12 oz.) mushrooms
40 g (1$\frac{1}{2}$ oz.) butter
40 g (1$\frac{1}{2}$ oz.) flour
125 ml ($\frac{1}{4}$ pint) milk
Salt, pepper, and a pinch of paprika
2 tablespoons cream

Rinse the mushrooms. Cut them into thin slices. Melt the butter in a saucepan. Add the mushrooms and fry them over a medium heat for 3–5 minutes until tender. Sprinkle over the flour and mix gently. Add the milk and stir gently over a medium heat until the sauce is thick and smooth. Season with salt, pepper, and a pinch of paprika. Stir in the cream and leave to cool. Fill the croustades with the mushroom mixture. Reheat them in a medium oven (190 C., 375 F., Reg. 5) for 5 minutes or until hot through.

2. *Creamed Salt Beef with Mushrooms*

200 g (8 oz.) cooked salt beef or brisket, chopped
100 g (4 oz.) mushrooms
40 g (1½ oz.) butter
40 g (1½ oz.) flour
125 ml (¼ pint) milk
Salt and pepper
½ teaspoon mushroom ketchup
2 tablespoons cream
Chopped parsley

Cut and shred the beef into small pieces. Wash, dry and chop the mushrooms. Melt the butter in a saucepan. Add the mushrooms and cook them for 3 minutes over a medium heat. Sprinkle with the flour and mix gently. Add the milk and stir gently over a medium heat until the sauce is thick and smooth. Add the meat to the sauce. Season with salt, pepper, and ½ teaspoon mushroom ketchup. Mix well. Add the cream. Leave to cool. Fill the croustades with the meat mixture. Reheat in a medium oven (190 C., 375 F., Reg. 5) for 5 minutes or until hot through. Sprinkle over the chopped parsley before serving.

Note: Any creamed filling may be used for croustades. See also fillings for vol au vent.

Tuna and Anchovy Flan

100 g (4 oz.) plain flour
Salt and pepper
50 g (2 oz.) butter
1 egg
1 tablespoon iced water
1 large tin tuna
40 g (1½ oz.) butter
40 g (1½ oz.) flour
250 ml (½ pint) milk

2 teaspoons lemon juice
1 tablespoon mixed chopped chives and parsley
1 small tin anchovy fillets

Sieve the flour with some salt and pepper onto a wooden board or marble slab. Make a well in the centre. Cut the 50 g (2 oz.) butter into small pieces and place it with the egg and water in the well. Gradually mix the flour into the butter, egg and water using the tips of the fingers. Form the pastry into a ball and chill it for at least an hour before rolling it out. Roll out the pastry as thinly as possible on a floured board, and line a 23 cm (9 inch) flan tin. Prick the bottom of the flan with a fork. Place a circle of waxed paper over the pastry. Fill it with dried peas, beans or rice. Bake the unfilled pastry case in a medium oven (190 C., 375 F., Reg. 5) for 15–20 minutes, until golden and crisp.

Carefully remove the paper and dried peas from the flan. Leave to cool.

Melt the 40 g (1½ oz.) butter in a saucepan. Add the 40 g (1½ oz.) flour and mix well. Gradually blend in the milk, stirring continually over a medium heat until the sauce boils and is thick and smooth. Drain the tuna and flake the meat with a fork. Add the tuna to the sauce. Season with salt and pepper and cook for 2 minutes. Remove from the heat and beat in the lemon juice and the chopped herbs. Pour the mixture into the flan case. Arrange the anchovy fillets on the surface. Heat through in a fairly hot oven (200 C., 400 F., Reg. 6) for 5–8 minutes. Serve hot.

SAVOURY PANCAKES

These pancakes form an inexpensive basis for a number of fillings varying from the exotic to the economical, depending on your budget. Whatever the stuffing, but provided they are thinly and evenly made, the pancakes make a delicious dish and have the great advantage of being able to be made well ahead of the meal and reheated in the oven. They also freeze successfully.

The secret of making perfect pancakes lies in using the right kind of pan and the right consistency of batter. The pan should be one that you keep entirely for omelettes and pancakes, preferably made of cast iron. It should have a thick, flat base with moulded edges and should never be washed or scrubbed on the inside. Clean the pan with a soft dry cloth or kitchen paper. The batter should have the consistency of very thin cream. If you find your pancakes are too thick, thin the batter with more milk or water. Cook the pancakes in an ungreased pan. The melted butter in the batter provides enough fat to prevent them from sticking.

Pancake Batter for 12 Pancakes

150 g (6 oz.) plain flour
2 eggs
375 ml ($\frac{3}{4}$ pint) milk
4 tablespoons melted butter
Salt and pepper

Sift the flour into a bowl. Make a well in the centre. Break the eggs into the well and beat them into the flour with a wooden spoon. Gradually beat in the milk and finish with a wire whisk or rotary beater until the batter is smooth. Season with salt and pepper and mix in the melted butter.

The batter should stand for an hour before use but this is not absolutely necessary.

Heat the ungreased pan and pour in about 1$\frac{1}{2}$ tablespoons of the batter. Tilt the pan so that the batter spreads evenly. Cook the pancake over a medium heat for 1 minute until golden brown. Flip it over and cook for a further minute on the other side. Stack the pancakes on top of each other until they are required.

Savoury Pancakes with Creamed Mushrooms

12 pancakes
200 g ($\frac{1}{2}$ lb.) mushrooms
40 g ($1\frac{1}{2}$ oz.) butter
1 small finely chopped onion
40 g ($1\frac{1}{2}$ oz.) flour
250 ml ($\frac{1}{2}$ pint) single cream
1 tablespoon sherry
Salt and freshly ground black pepper
50 g (2 oz.) grated cheese

Make the pancakes as shown above. Wash and slice the mushrooms through the caps and stalks. Melt the butter in a saucepan. Add the mushrooms and onion and cook over a medium heat for 5 minutes. Stir in the flour and mix well. Gradually add the cream, stirring continually until thick and smooth. Season with salt and pepper and stir in the sherry. Fill the pancakes with the mushroom mixture. Roll up neatly and arrange them in a shallow dish. Sprinkle the cheese over the top. Bake in a hot oven (220 C., 425 F., Reg. 7) for 10–12 minutes until golden brown. Serve hot.

Savoury Pancakes with Left-Over Meat or Poultry

12 pancakes
300 g (12 oz.) minced cooked chicken, ham or beef
25 g (1 oz.) butter
1 small chopped onion
25 g (1 oz.) flour
250 ml ($\frac{1}{2}$ pint) milk
Salt and freshly ground black pepper

Make the pancakes as shown on page 185 and keep them warm. Melt the butter in a saucepan. Add the onion and cook over a medium heat until the onion is soft. Add the flour and mix well. Gradually add the milk, stirring continually until the sauce is thick and smooth. Season with plenty of salt and freshly ground black pepper and mix in the minced meat. Fill the pancakes with the mixture. Roll up neatly and arrange in a shallow dish. Heat through in a medium oven (190 C., 375 F., Reg. 5) for 5 minutes. Serve hot.

Note: The sauce may be varied by the addition of tomato purée, a dash of Worcester sauce or finely chopped parsley.

Savoury Pancakes with Prawns

12 pancakes
200 g (½ lb.) fresh prawns
1 tablespoon chopped chives
25 g (1 oz.) butter
25 g (1 oz.) flour
250 ml (½ pint) milk
Salt and pepper
1 egg yolk, beaten
1 tablespoon sherry or vermouth
1 teaspoon lemon juice
50 g (2 oz.) grated cheese

Make the pancakes as shown on page 185. Shell the prawns and remove the black vein. Cut them into small pieces and mix them with the chopped chives. Melt the butter in a saucepan. Add the flour and mix well. Gradually add the milk, stirring continually, until the sauce is thick and smooth. Add the prawns and chives to the sauce. Season with salt and pepper. Remove from the heat and stir in the egg yolk, sherry or vermouth, and lemon juice.

Fill the pancakes with the prawn mixture. Roll up neatly and arrange in a shallow baking dish. Sprinkle with cheese and bake in a hot oven (220 C., 425 F., Reg. 7) for 10–12 minutes until golden brown. Serve hot.

CHAPTER ELEVEN

EGGS & CHEESE

EGGS

BAKED EGGS (OEUFS EN COCOTTE)

Baked eggs are undoubtedly one of the miracles of cookery. They can be served as a first course for lunch or dinner, as a snack at any time and as a good filler for supper or high tea. Eggs cooked in this way lend themselves to a hundred different ways of serving. A few of them are included in this book and the rest you can invent for yourself with the contents of the larder and the refrigerator and with any left-overs of meat, fish and vegetables that are around.

With baked eggs the degree of cooking is very important. They should be baked until the whites are just set – not slimy – and the yolks are firm but not hard and rubbery. They must be served in fireproof cocottes or ramekin dishes. These can be bought in Woolworths and are also useful for baking individual soufflés and for sweets. The eggs should be served at once as they go on cooking once they are taken from the oven. Serve them on a shallow dish covered with a clean white napkin.

To Cook Baked Eggs
    4 eggs
    4 tablespoons cream
    15 g ($\frac{1}{2}$ oz.) butter
    Salt and freshly ground black pepper
    Fireproof cocottes or ramekin dishes

Butter the cocottes and place them in a roasting tin half filled with boiling water. Break an egg into each dish, cover with 1 tablespoon cream. Sprinkle the eggs with salt and pepper and place a quarter of the butter on each one. Bake in a moderate oven (180 C., 350 F., Reg. 4) for 6–10 minutes until set.

Serve at once with hot toast, French bread or garlic bread (see page 227).

Baked Eggs with Ham

4 eggs
4 tablespoons cream
100 g (4 oz.) ham
15 g (½ oz.) butter
Salt and freshly ground pepper
Fireproof cocottes or ramekin dishes

Butter the cocottes and place them in a roasting tin half filled with boiling water. Chop the ham and place some in the bottom of each dish. Break the eggs over the ham and cover with a spoonful of cream. Sprinkle with salt and pepper and place a quarter of the butter on the top of each one. Bake in a moderate oven (180 C., 350 F., Reg. 4) for 6–10 minutes until the eggs are set.

Serve at once.

Variations: Replace the ham with
  1. 100 g (4 oz.) chopped tongue
  2. 100 g (4 oz.) chopped smoked salmon
  3. 100 g (4 oz.) grated cheese
  4. 100 g (4 oz.) potted shrimps or peeled prawns
  5. 100 g (4 oz.) fresh or tinned crabmeat
  6. 150 g (6 oz.) fresh or tinned mushrooms, finely chopped
      and fried in 15 g (½ oz.) butter
  7. 1 small tin pâté

HARD BOILED EGGS

Hard boiled eggs are used in many hot and cold dishes. Peel

the eggs as soon as they are cooked and keep them covered by warm or cold water until they are to be used.

Use only fresh eggs for hard boiling. If they have been kept in a refrigerator or a cool place, allow them to reach room temperature before putting them into the boiling water as this prevents them from cracking.

To cook Hard Boiled Eggs. Plunge eggs into fast boiling salted water and cook for 15 minutes. Cool the eggs under cold running water and remove the shells. Cut hard boiled eggs with an egg cutter or with a knife dipped in water.

Egg Mayonnaise

6 eggs
Lettuce leaves
250 ml ($\frac{1}{2}$ pint) mayonnaise
1 tablespoon double cream
2 teaspoons capers
4 anchovy fillets

Boil the eggs in salted water for 15 minutes. Cool them under cold running water and shell. Cut them in half lengthwise and arrange them white side up, on a bed of lettuce leaves. Add the cream to the mayonnaise and spoon over the eggs so that they are well covered. Decorate with capers and anchovy fillets.

Serve chilled with thin slices of buttered brown bread.

Variations
1. Add a tablespoon of chopped chives to the mayonnaise.
2. Add 50 g (2 oz.) peeled prawns to the mayonnaise. Garnish with thin strips of tinned pimento.
3. Add 2 teaspoons of curry paste, mixed with a little lemon juice, to the mayonnaise. Garnish with a few thin slices of tomato.
4. Add a tablespoon of tomato purée to the mayonnaise. Garnish with anchovies.

Eggs in Green Mayonnaise

6 hard boiled eggs
Lettuce leaves
4 sprigs parsley
4 sprigs tarragon
100 g (¼ lb.) spinach
½ bunch watercress
250 ml (½ pint) mayonnaise
1 tablespoon cream

Cut the shelled eggs in half lengthwise and arrange them, cut sides down, on a bed of shredded lettuce. Chop the parsley, tarragon, spinach and watercress, discarding the stalks. Cook in fast boiling salted water for 3 minutes. Drain well and rub through a fine sieve. Add the purée to the mayonnaise. Mix in the cream and spoon over the eggs so that they are well covered.
Serve chilled.

Stuffed Anchovy Eggs

6 hard boiled eggs
1 tin anchovy fillets
50 g (2 oz.) softened butter
Freshly ground black pepper
2 firm tomatoes

Soak the anchovies in milk for 10 minutes to remove excess saltiness. Drain well and chop finely. Cut the eggs in half lengthwise. Remove the yolks and mash them with the butter. Add the chopped anchovies, mix well and season with freshly ground black pepper. Stuff the egg whites with the mixture. Arrange the eggs on a dish and decorate with thin slices of tomato.
Serve chilled with buttered slices of brown bread.

Mimosa Eggs

6 hard boiled eggs
1 teaspoon Dijon mustard
125 ml ($\frac{1}{4}$ pint) mayonnaise
2 tablespoons mixed chopped parsley, tarragon, and chervil
Lettuce leaves
Salt and pepper

Cut the shelled eggs in half lengthwise and remove the yolks. Mash four of the egg yolks with a fork and mix them with the mustard, the mayonnaise, the finely chopped herbs, and some salt and pepper. Fill the egg whites with the mayonnaise mixture and arrange them on a serving plate on a bed of crisp lettuce leaves. Rub the remaining egg yolks through a sieve and sprinkle over the stuffed eggs.

Serve chilled with thin slices of buttered brown bread.

Hard Boiled Eggs with an Onion Sauce

6 hard boiled eggs
75 g (3 oz.) butter
25 g (1 oz.) flour
250 ml ($\frac{1}{2}$ pint) milk
2 tablespoons cream
2 medium onions
Salt and pepper
A pinch of nutmeg

Cut the hard boiled eggs into quarters and arrange them in a shallow fireproof serving dish. Melt 50 g (2 oz.) of butter in a saucepan. Add the flour and mix well. Gradually mix in the milk, stirring continually over a medium heat until the sauce is thick and smooth. Bring to the boil and cook for 2 minutes. Reduce the heat and mix in the cream. Do not boil again. Season with salt, pepper and a pinch of nutmeg.

Peel and chop the onions and fry until soft in 25 g (1 oz.)

butter. Mix the onions into the sauce and pour over the hard boiled eggs. Reheat the dish in a medium oven (190 C., 375 F., Reg. 5) for 5–8 minutes until hot through. Serve at once.

Hard Boiled Eggs in a Mustard Sauce

6 hard boiled eggs
3 thin rashers of bacon
40 g (1½ oz.) butter
40 g (1½ oz.) flour
2 tablespoons Dijon mustard
375 ml (¾ pint) milk
1 tablespoon cream
1 egg yolk
Salt and pepper

Peel and chop the eggs. Fry the bacon until crisp. Remove the rind and break into small pieces. Melt the butter in a saucepan. Add the flour and mix well. Gradually add the milk, stirring continually over a moderate heat, until the sauce is thick and smooth. Add the mustard to the sauce. Bring to the boil and cook for 3 minutes. Remove the sauce from the heat. Beat the cream with the egg yolk. Mix it with the sauce. Season with salt and pepper. Add the chopped eggs to the sauce. Heat through but do not boil. Arrange in a serving dish. Sprinkle over the bacon.

Serve hot with garlic or cheese bread (see page 227).

Stuffed Eggs with Watercress Salad

6 hard boiled eggs
2 bunches watercress
1 tablespoon lemon juice
Salt and freshly ground black pepper
50 g (2 oz.) butter
½ teaspoon curry powder
1 anchovy fillet

Cut the eggs in half lengthwise and remove the yolks. Remove any tough stalks from the watercress. Toss it in the lemon juice and season with salt and pepper. Mix the egg yolks with the butter and the curry powder. Beat until smooth. Chop the anchovy fillet very, very finely and mix with the egg yolks and butter. Season with salt and pepper. Fill the egg whites with the yolk mixture and sandwich the two halves together.

Cut the whole eggs into thin slices with a knife dipped in cold water or in an egg slicer. Arrange the slices on the watercress. Serve chilled.

Curried Eggs

Cold curried eggs are delicious. We often have them on picnics but they are also delicious served as a first course.

6 hard boiled eggs
25 g (1 oz.) butter
1 small onion
1½ tablespoons flour
250 ml (½ pint) hot milk or stock
1 teaspoon curry powder
4 tablespoons sultanas or seedless raisins
Salt and pepper
Chopped parsley

Cut the eggs in half and place them cut side down in a shallow dish. Peel the onion and cut it into thin slices. Melt the butter in a saucepan. Add the onion and cook over a gentle flame until it is soft and tender, about 5 minutes. Blend in the flour and curry powder and mix well. Gradually add the hot milk or stock, stirring continually until the sauce is thick and smooth. Cook for 5 minutes over a medium heat. Add the sultanas and continue to cook for a further 5 minutes. Season with salt and pepper. Pour the sauce over the eggs and leave to cool.

Serve cold, garnished with chopped parsley.
Note: Bombay duck (dried salt fish), which can be bought

in delicatessen shops, gives an air of professionalism to this dish. Soak the Bombay duck, then dry well and fry in deep oil until crisp. Break into small pieces and sprinkle over the dish.

Garlic Eggs

6 hard boiled eggs
4 cloves of garlic
2 anchovy fillets
2 teaspoons capers
3 tablespoons olive oil
1 teaspoon white wine vinegar
Salt and freshly ground black pepper

Cut the eggs into slices or quarters. Chop and crush the garlic or put it through a garlic press. Add the anchovy fillets and the capers to the garlic and mash with a fork to make a thick paste. Blend in the olive oil, add the vinegar and season with salt and pepper. Spread the mixture over the eggs.
Chill before serving.

OEUFS MOLLETS
Many egg dishes are prepared by using whole peeled soft boiled eggs in the place of hard boiled or poached eggs. They are more easily digested than hard boiled eggs and less trouble to prepare than poached eggs. The eggs are boiled for 5 minutes in salted water and then immediately plunged under cold running water before being shelled. They can be served with either a hot or cold sauce.

Oeufs Mollets Robert

4 eggs
50 g (2 oz.) butter
2 finely chopped onions
25 g (1 oz.) flour
250 ml ($\frac{1}{2}$ pint) brown stock
1 teaspoon red wine vinegar

1 tablespoon Dijon mustard
Salt and pepper

Cook the eggs as for oeufs mollets (above) and put each one in a ramekin dish. Melt the butter in a saucepan. Add the onions and cook them over a medium heat until they are soft and transparent. Add the flour and stir well. Gradually add the stock and vinegar, mixing well. Simmer the sauce over a low heat for 10 minutes. Add the mustard and season with salt and pepper. Pour the hot sauce over the eggs and serve at once.

Oeufs Mollets Delphine

4 eggs
50 g (2 oz.) ham
50 g (2 oz.) butter
1 tablespoon flour
125 ml ($\frac{1}{4}$ pint) cream
$\frac{1}{2}$ tablespoon chopped parsley
$\frac{1}{2}$ tablespoon chopped chives or spring onions
Salt and pepper

Cook the eggs as for oeufs mollets (above). Chop the ham into small dice. Cover the bottom of 4 individual ramekin dishes with the chopped ham and place the eggs on top. Melt the butter in a saucepan. Add the flour and stir over a medium heat until thoroughly blended. Stir in the cream, chopped parsley and chives and season with salt and pepper. Continue to stir over a low heat until the sauce is thick and smooth.
Pour the sauce over the eggs and serve immediately.

POACHED EGGS
Eggs poached in almost boiling water must be treated with the utmost gentleness. If you are nervous, poach them in a special 'egg poacher', four metal moulds which fit into a pan and are covered by a lid – but the taste is not the same! The perfect poached egg is oval in shape, the white is pure white and like jelly, the yolk is just set but never hard.

To Poach Eggs
   4 eggs
   Salted water

Use a shallow saucepan, half fill it with salted water and bring to the boil. Break one egg into a cup. Reduce the heat slightly, swirl the water in a whirlpool with a spoon and drop the egg gently into the pan. Use a large spoon to scoop water over it to cook the surface. The water should be just bubbling. As soon as the yolk is firm, remove it with an egg slice and keep it warm on a heated plate if it is to be used in hot dishes, or slip it into a shallow dish of cold water if it is to be used for cold dishes. More than one egg can be cooked at a time but take care not to let them touch too much.

Trim any untidy edges off the eggs with scissors or with a pastry-cutter.

Poached Eggs Florentine

   800 g (2 lb.) fresh spinach, or 1 large tin puréed spinach, or
      1 large packet frozen spinach
   50 g (2 oz.) butter
   4 eggs
   25 g (1 oz.) flour
   250 ml ($\frac{1}{2}$ pint) milk
   Salt and pepper
   2 tablespoons cream
   50 g (2 oz.) grated Gruyère or Parmesan cheese

Trim off the tough stems from the spinach and cook the rest in a very little boiling salted water until tender, about 10–15 minutes. Drain well and purée through a fine sieve or food mill, or in an electric blender. Stir 25 g (1 oz.) butter into the spinach purée and season with a little salt and pepper. Arrange in a fireproof serving dish, making four wells in the spinach. Poach the eggs until set in nearly boiling water. Remove the eggs from the water with a slotted spoon and slide them into the wells in the spinach.

Melt 25 g (1 oz.) butter in a saucepan, add the flour and mix well. Gradually blend in the milk stirring continually over a medium heat until the sauce is thick and smooth. Season with salt and pepper. Add the cream and half the cheese to the sauce. Continue to cook until the cheese has melted. *Do not boil.* Pour the sauce over the eggs and spinach. Sprinkle over the remaining cheese and bake in a fairly hot oven (200 C., 400 F., Reg. 6) until golden brown. Serve hot.

Note: The eggs can be cooked in individual dishes.

Eggs Benedict

A popular American dish which has to be made at the last minute.

4 slices of bread
4 slices of ham
4 poached eggs
125 ml ($\frac{1}{4}$ pint) hollandaise sauce (see page 214)

Toast the bread and cut it into 6 cm ($2\frac{1}{2}$ inch) rounds, with a pastry-cutter if you have one. Spread each slice with butter. Cut the ham into 6 cm ($2\frac{1}{2}$ inch) rounds and place it over the toast. Poach the eggs in nearly boiling water for 3–4 minutes. Remove them with an egg slice and trim any untidy edges. Place the eggs on the ham and spoon over the hot hollandaise sauce. Serve at once. Follow with a light main course.

Yellow Sunset

Please don't be frightened by the idea of cold scrambled eggs. *They are delicious!* This particular combination is cool and pretty to look at.

8 eggs
65 g ($2\frac{1}{2}$ oz.) butter
1 tablespoon milk or cream
Salt and freshly ground black pepper
200 g (8 oz.) smoked pork loin, cut into thin slices

Melt 40 g (1½ oz.) butter in a small thick bottomed saucepan. Beat the eggs lightly with the milk or cream and season with salt and pepper. Pour the eggs into the pan and cook over a gentle heat, stirring occasionally and not too vigorously, until the eggs are just set. Remove from heat; stir in 25 g (1 oz.) butter cut into small pieces. Spoon the scrambled egg into an oblong mould. Leave to set in a cool place. Turn out and cut into thin slices.

Arrange alternate slices of cold scrambled eggs and smoked pork fillet on 4 plates. Serve chilled with hot toast and butter.

Variation: Replace the pork with 200 g (8 oz.) smoked eel fillet.

SOUFFLÉS

Add very stiffly beaten whites of eggs to a thick mixture bound by egg yolks, bake it and you have a miracle called a soufflé. The mixture doubles its size in the oven and becomes a light, airy and melting delicacy.

A soufflé is not difficult to make but it does have to be served at *exactly* the right moment. If the soufflé is not the right consistency but is either too dry or too runny, it will swiftly lose its amazing height and collapse into a sorry wrinkled puddle at the bottom of the dish once it is removed from the oven. Overcooked it will dry out in the centre, losing its flavour and texture.

Making a Soufflé
1. Grease well a soufflé dish or round dish with straight sides.
2. Whisk the egg whites until they are really stiff – you should be able to turn the bowl upside down without the whites moving. Fold them gently into the base sauce mixture, using a fork.
3. Place the soufflé immediately into a pre-heated oven. Close the door and do not open it until the time specified. A sudden draught can cause the soufflé to sink.
4. Serve the soufflé straight from the oven onto hot plates.

Note: The soufflé base can be made well in advance so that last minute preparation only involves the beating and folding in of the egg whites. It is also possible to get reasonable results by actually folding in the stiffly beaten whites of eggs in advance and leaving the soufflé in the freezing compartment of the refrigerator for up to 2 hours. In this case an extra ten minutes should be added to the cooking time.

Greek Courgette Soufflé

800 g (2 lbs.) courgettes
100 g (4 oz.) melted butter
150 g (6 oz.) grated Cheddar or Parmesan cheese
Salt and pepper
A pinch of nutmeg
3 egg yolks
4 egg whites

Butter a soufflé dish. Wash and slice the courgettes. Cook them in boiling salted water for 20 minutes or until they are tender. Drain them well and pat them dry with kitchen paper. Purée the courgettes through a sieve, in an electric blender or through a food mill. Mix the melted butter, the cheese and the egg yolks into the courgette purée. Season with salt, pepper and a pinch of nutmeg.

Whip the egg whites until stiff. Fold them gently into the courgette mixture. Pour the mixture into the soufflé dish. Bake in a medium oven (190 C., 375 F., Reg. 5) for 30 minutes. Serve at once, with a tomato sauce (see page 220).

Individual Cheese Soufflés

100 g (¼ lb.) butter
50 g (2 oz.) flour
500 ml (1 pint) milk
1 teaspoonful made English mustard
Salt and pepper
4 eggs
100 g (¼ lb.) grated Gruyère or Cheddar cheese

Melt the butter in a saucepan. Add the flour and mix well until the mixture forms a ball and leaves the side of the pan.

Gradually stir in the milk and cook over a medium heat until the mixture is thick and smooth. Stir in the mustard. Remove from the heat and leave to cool. Separate the egg yolks from the whites. Beat three of the yolks one by one into the mixture until each one has blended in. Add the grated cheese and mix well. Season with salt and pepper. Beat the egg whites until stiff, fold them gently into the cheese mixture, using a fork. Pour into buttered ramekins being careful not to fill each one more than half full. Bake for 20 minutes in a medium oven (190 C., 375 F., Reg. 5). Serve immediately.

CHEESE

Croque Monsieur

My own version of the savoury cheese and ham sandwich, adapted to serve as a first course.

6 slices white bread
2 eggs
Salt and pepper
125 g (5 oz.) butter
25 g (1 oz.) flour
250 ml ($\frac{1}{2}$ pint) milk
100 g (4 oz.) grated Cheddar or Gruyère cheese
50 g (2 oz.) chopped ham

Cut the slices of bread into twelve 5 cm (2 inch) circles with a pastry cutter. Beat the eggs and season with salt and pepper. Dip the bread into the beaten egg and fry until crisp and golden in about 75 g (3 oz.) butter. Keep warm. Melt 50 g (2 oz.) butter in a saucepan, add the flour and mix well. Gradually blend in the milk, stirring continually over a medium heat until the sauce is thick and smooth. Bring to the boil and mix in 50 g (2 oz.) of the grated cheese. Spread the sauce over the fried slices of bread. Cover with chopped ham and sprinkle over the remaining 50 g (2 oz.) grated cheese.

Place the slices on a baking sheet and bake in a hot oven (230 C., 450 F., Reg. 8) for 5–8 minutes until golden brown. Serve at once.

Iced Camembert

    1 ripe Camembert cheese
    75 g (3 oz.) softened butter
    2 tablespoons dry white wine
    125 ml ($\frac{1}{4}$ pint) double cream
    Salt and pepper
    2 tablespoons grated Parmesan cheese
    Paprika pepper
    Watercress

Remove the skin from the Camembert, scraping it to get off all the cheese. Mash the cheese and the butter together with a fork. Add the wine and beat until smooth. Season with salt and pepper and add the double cream. Turn the cheese into a lightly oiled mould. Chill in the ice compartment of a refrigerator for $1\frac{1}{2}$–2 hours. Turn out, sprinkle with the Parmesan cheese and garnish with paprika and watercress. Serve iced with hot salt biscuits or hot toast.

Summer Salad

As a first course for a summer lunch or a hot evening this is a light and attractive mixture involving no cooking. Perfect for slimmers!

    100 g (4 oz.) Cheddar cheese
    8 small firm tomatoes
    50 g (2 oz.) sultanas
    12 seedless grapes
    $\frac{1}{2}$ green pepper
    2 crisp eating apples
    2 tablespoons Boursin or cream cheese
    3 tablespoons olive oil
    1 tablespoon white wine vinegar
    Salt and freshly ground black pepper

Grate the Cheddar cheese. Quarter the tomatoes. Core and

seed the pepper. Chop it finely. Peel, core, and dice the apples. Arrange the Cheddar in the centre of a serving dish. Surround with the tomato quarters. Sprinkle over the grapes and sultanas, chopped pepper and diced apple.

Combine the Boursin or cream cheese with the olive oil and vinegar. Season with salt and pepper. Pour the dressing over the salad. Serve chilled.

Note: Triangles of bread crisply fried in bacon fat go deliciously with this dish – for the non-slimmers of course!

CHAPTER TWELVE

USING TINNED SOUPS

It is an unfortunate fact that the more expensive the soup the better the taste and quality. Cheap tinned soups have a rough taste about them and the thicker varieties have a distinct flavour of flour. Tinned soups are usually under-seasoned.

However it is possible to titivate the cheaper soups to make them passable and sometimes very good indeed. On the whole only three quarters of the quantity needed should be tinned soup, and the required amount should be made up by adding home-made stock (or a stock cube and water), milk, cream, cooked vegetables, cooked meat, sherry, vermouth, etc.

A GUIDE TO IMPROVING TINNED SOUPS

To Tomato Soup
Add puréed tinned tomatoes, tomato purée, milk and cream, lemon juice, sherry, and a pinch of sage or sweet basil.

To Vegetable Soup
Add stock, sherry, and fresh finely chopped cooked vegetables.

To Creamed Vegetable Soups
Add cream, chopped chives and parsley, chopped tinned mushrooms, asparagus, etc.

To Creamed Chicken Soup
Add cooked chopped chicken, lemon juice, cream, chopped parsley, and paprika pepper.

To Meat Soups
Add stock, sherry, Worcester and Tabasco sauce, and chopped cooked meat.

Expensive Tinned Soups
These, such as real turtle, or shark's fin, should be served as directed on the labels.

Using Packaged Soups
Follow the same plan as tinned soups, but remember that packaged soups are usually inclined to be highly seasoned, especially with salt.

Using Stock Cubes for Soup Making
It is not always possible to have home made stock at hand. Luckily stock cubes make a good alternative and there are two or three good varieties of beef and chicken stock cubes on the market. I prefer Knorr Swiss which I dilute by a little less than recommended on the packet. Like packaged soups, stock cubes are inclined to be salty.

CHAPTER THIRTEEN

QUICKIES

Quick Iced Crab Bisque

2 tins condensed tomato soup
125 ml ($\frac{1}{4}$ pint) cream
Salt and pepper
2 teaspoons lemon juice
Worcester and Tabasco sauce
1 tin crabmeat

Dilute the soup according to the instructions. Heat through. Season with salt, pepper, lemon juice and a few drops of Worcester and Tabasco sauce. Add the drained and flaked crabmeat and cook for 3 minutes over a medium heat. Leave to cool. Stir in the cream and chill well before serving.

Quick Iced Borsch

1 tin consommé
1 tin beetroot
2 teaspoons lemon juice
Salt and pepper
Cream and chopped chives
Whipped cream

Put the tinned beetroot through a fine sieve, a food mill or an electric liquidizer. Combine the beetroot and beetroot juice and the consommé. Stir in the lemon juice. Season with salt and pepper.

Serve well chilled with a spoonful of whipped cream and chopped chives on each serving.

Quick Iced Tomato Soup

792 g (28 oz.) tin Italian tomatoes
1 tin consommé
Salt and pepper
Sherry
1 teaspoon sugar
Grated rind of 1 orange
Chopped chives

Put the tomatoes through a fine sieve or food mill, or blend in an electric liquidizer. Combine the tomato purée, consommé, sherry and the orange rind in a saucepan. Season with salt, pepper and sugar. Heat gently and simmer uncovered for 10 minutes. Cool and serve well chilled, garnished with chopped chives.

Iced Tuna Cloud

For quick preparation this dish is hard to beat. Serve it in hot weather, piled in glass dishes.

1 tin consommé
1 tin tuna fish
125 ml ($\frac{1}{4}$ pint) double cream
2 teaspoons lemon juice
Salt and pepper
A few drops of Tabasco sauce

Drain the tuna fish. Flake the flesh with a fork. Mix the tuna with the consommé and chill in the ice-making compartment of the refrigerator until set. Break up the jelly and tuna fish with a fork. Mix in the lemon juice. Season with salt, pepper and a few drops of Tabasco sauce. Whip the cream and fold it lightly into the tuna mixture.
   Pile into glass dishes and serve chilled.

Prawns with Potato Salad

1 tin fancy prawns
1 small tin Heinz potato salad
Freshly ground black pepper
Lettuce or tomato slices for garnish
Paprika pepper

Drain the prawns and mix them with the potato salad. Season
with pepper and arrange on a bed of lettuce leaves or on a
plate garnished with slices of tomato. Sprinkle the salad with
a little dusting of paprika and chill before serving.

Tomato Juice Cocktail

A sophisticated version of the British Railways way of serving
tomato juice.

500 ml (1 pint) tinned or bottled tomato juice
2 tablespoons sherry
1 teaspoon lemon juice
Celery salt
Freshly ground black pepper
Few drops of Worcester sauce
1 lemon for garnish

Combine all the ingredients together and mix well. Chill and
serve in individual glasses with a little crushed ice, garnished
with a very thin slice of lemon.

CHAPTER FOURTEEN

SAUCES

It is in the field of sauces that the great professional chefs really come into their own. They revel in the long preparations of complicated concoctions involving lengthy pounding, sieving and mixing, where a dozen or so ingredients go to make up one little sauce. I have left out that kind as I seldom have time to make them in my kitchen, and I doubt if many other housewives do either.

Don't imagine I underestimate the importance of sauces – the very opposite. After all, the addition of a sauce can make the simplest of dishes a culinary masterpiece. Take eggs Benedict for instance, which without the hollandaise sauce are merely poached eggs on slices of ham, served on pieces of toast. Pour over the hollandaise and you have one of the most delicious dishes invented. However, it is a mistake to feel that a sauce covers all defects. A piece of overbaked fish which has lost its taste and texture will not be greatly improved by adding a sauce, however good it is.

The sauces in this book are all easy to make and a valuable asset to the range of first courses. Seasoning is very much a matter of taste; to suit everyone I have kept it to a basic minimum thereby leaving room for any additions you wish to make yourself. I often add a drop of Tabasco sauce to a plain mayonnaise and on the whole I add more lemon juice than stated in the recipes.

I have divided the sauces into four main groups: emulsions, salad dressings, cold, and hot.

Classic French Mayonnaise

Every competent cook has an individual method of making mayonnaise. Some swear by an electric whisk or rotary beater. I find a wooden spoon far the best implement to use, but whichever method you employ, two things are essential. The ingredients must all be at the same temperature and the olive oil must be added to the egg yolks in very small quantities.

I place the bowl I am using on a damp cloth to prevent it moving and beat with my right hand, dribbling in the oil from a small jug in my left hand. The following method makes just over 250 ml ($\frac{1}{2}$ pint) of mayonnaise.

> 2 egg yolks
> 250 ml ($\frac{1}{2}$ pint) olive oil
> 2 teaspoons lemon juice or white wine vinegar
> Salt and pepper

Make sure that there is no egg white adhering to the yolks. Place the yolks in a clean bowl and beat them well with a wooden spoon. Adding only a few drops at a time, beat the olive oil into the egg yolks. Never add more oil until the preceding drops have been completely absorbed into the yolks. When the sauce becomes very thick and gluey, the olive oil can be added in a thin stream. When all the olive oil has been absorbed, beat in the vinegar and season with salt and pepper.

Keep the mayonnaise in a cool place, but not in a refrigerator, until required.

Note: For a stronger tasting mayonnaise, add 1 teaspoon mustard to the yolks before adding the oil.

CURDLED MAYONNAISE. If the mayonnaise should curdle beat a fresh egg yolk in a clean bowl. Add the curdled mixture, drop by drop, beating constantly.

Mayonnaise curdles:
1. if the olive oil is added too fast,

2. if the vinegar or lemon juice is added before the yolks and oil are properly emulsified,
3. if the egg yolks and oil are at different temperatures, i.e. if the egg is taken from the refrigerator and the oil from the kitchen cupboard.
4. if the weather is thundery,
5. according to old wives' tales, if you yourself are feeling under the weather!

Dill Mayonnaise

Add 2 teaspoons finely chopped fresh dill to the egg yolks before beating in the oil. This is particularly good with cold white fish.

Garlic Mayonnaise or Aïoli Sauce

Pound 3 cloves of garlic in a pestle and mortar and mix them with the egg yolks before adding the oil.

Herb Mayonnaise

Add 2 teaspoons mixed finely chopped chives, parsley, chervil, and tarragon.

Tomato Mayonnaise

A pretty pink colour and good with fish. Beat in 1 tablespoon of tomato purée or paste when the mayonnaise is made.

Curried Mayonnaise

This takes a bit of time but is worth doing. The mayonnaise goes well with cold fish, shellfish, chicken and eggs.

25 g (1 oz.) butter
1 small onion
2 tablespoons curry powder

1 teaspoon flour
4 tomatoes
125 ml ($\frac{1}{4}$ pint) chicken stock made with $\frac{1}{2}$ cube
$\frac{1}{2}$ teaspoon sugar
2 tablespoons cream
125 ml ($\frac{1}{4}$ pint) mayonnaise (see page 210)
1 teaspoon lemon juice (optional)

Peel and chop the onion. Chop the tomatoes.

Melt the butter in a saucepan. Add the onion and cook over a medium heat until it is soft and transparent. Stir in the curry powder and flour and mix well. Add the tomatoes, stock and sugar. Bring to the boil and simmer for 20 minutes. Strain the mixture through a fine sieve and leave to cool. Add the curry mixture and the cream to the mayonnaise. Mix well and season with lemon juice if necessary.

Green Mayonnaise

250 ml ($\frac{1}{2}$ pint) mayonnaise (see page 210)
2 handfuls raw spinach
1 tablespoon French mustard

Wash the spinach and remove the stems. Plunge the leaves into fast boiling salted water and cook for 3 minutes. Drain well and squeeze any remaining water into a bowl. Chop the spinach very finely and mix well with the mayonnaise and mustard. Colour the mayonnaise with a little of the spinach juice. Keep in a cool place until required.

Russian Salad Sauce

125 ml ($\frac{1}{4}$ pint) mayonnaise (see page 210)
2 tablespoons red caviar
2 teaspoons lemon juice
1 teaspoon grated onion

Mix the red caviar, lemon juice, and onion with the mayonnaise. Serve with fish and shellfish.

Seafood Sauce

Use with cold shellfish, cold white fish fillets and with fish cocktails. This sauce also goes well with crisply fried fish.

250 ml ($\frac{1}{2}$ pint) mayonnaise (see page 210)
2 tablespoons tomato ketchup
2 tablespoons cream
A few drops of Worcester sauce
A few drops of Tabasco sauce
1 teaspoon lemon juice

Combine the mayonnaise with the tomato ketchup and cream. Season with Worcester sauce, Tabasco sauce and lemon juice. Serve chilled.

Sauce Tartare

250 ml ($\frac{1}{2}$ pint) mayonnaise (see page 210)
1 tablespoon French mustard
2 tablespoons capers
1 tablespoon gherkins

Mix the mustard with the mayonnaise. Chop very finely, or mince, the capers and gherkins. Mix into the mayonnaise. Keep in a cool place until required.
Serve with fried and cold fish.

Anchovy Salad Dressing

3 tablespoons mayonnaise (see page 210)
3 tablespoons sour cream
$\frac{1}{2}$ tin anchovy fillets, chopped
2 tablespoons chopped parsley
1 clove garlic (minced or pressed through a garlic press)

Combine all the ingredients and mix well. Serve with vegetable and fish salads.

Hollandaise Sauce

This sauce is made like a mayonnaise – very slowly. If it should curdle add a little boiling water and whisk vigorously.

4 egg yolks
150 g (6 oz.) softened unsalted butter
3 tablespoons boiling water
1 tablespoon lemon juice
Salt and white pepper

Place the egg yolks in the top of a double boiler over hot water (do not boil the water). Whisk the egg yolks with one table-spoon of the water for 3 minutes. Gradually whisk in the softened butter a teaspoon at a time allowing the butter and egg yolks to emulsify before each addition of more butter. When all the butter has been used, add the remaining water and the lemon juice. Season with salt and white pepper.
Serve at once with eggs, fish or boiled vegetables.
Note: If you wish to keep the sauce for a bit, cover it with a lid and leave it over warm water.

Sauce Mousseline

Hollandaise sauce (see above)
2 tablespoons double cream

Whip the cream and add to the hollandaise sauce. Serve with boiled or fried fish, boiled vegetables or soufflés.

Sauce Vinaigrette or French Dressing

3 tablespoons olive oil
1 tablespoon vinegar
Salt and freshly ground black pepper

Combine all the ingredients. Mix well by stirring, whisking or shaking in a screw top jar. Serve with salads, raw and cooked vegetables, fish and meat.

French dressing can also be made with mustard – add either 2 teaspoons Dijon mustard or 1 teaspoon dry English mustard to the above mixture.

Curry Dressing

French dressing (see page 214)
½ teaspoon grated onion
½ teaspoon curry paste or powder

Mix a little of the French dressing with the onion and curry until a smooth paste is formed. Add the rest of the dressing and mix well. Serve with poultry, fish and shellfish salads.

Onion Dressing

French dressing (see page 214)
2 teaspoons minced or grated onion

Mix the French dressing with the onion. Serve with vegetable, fish and meat salads.

Garlic Dressing

French dressing (see page 214)
1 clove garlic

Squeeze the garlic through a garlic press, or chop finely, or grind in a pestle and mortar. Add the French dressing and mix well. Serve with salads.

Blue Cheese Dressing

French dressing (see page 214)
25 g (1 oz.) soft blue cheese

Mix the blue cheese to a smooth paste with a little of the French dressing. Add the rest of the dressing and mix well. Serve with vegetable salads.

Cream Cheese Dressing

French dressing (see page 214)
25 g (1 oz.) cream cheese
1 tablespoon chopped chives
Paprika pepper

Add a little of the French dressing to the cream cheese. Mix to a smooth paste. Add the rest of the dressing. Season with paprika pepper and add chives. Serve with vegetable and tomato salads.

Tomato Dressing

French dressing (see page 214)
1 tablespoon tomato purée
½ teaspoon grated onion or 1 tablespoon chopped chives

Add a little of the French dressing to the tomato purée. Mix to a smooth paste and add the rest of the French dressing. Mix in the grated onion or chopped chives. Serve with vegetable, meat or fish salads.

Herb Dressing

French dressing (see page 214)
2 teaspoons mixed chopped chives, tarragon, and chervil

Combine the French dressing and herbs and mix well. Serve with salads.

Sharp French Dressing

French dressing (see page 214)
1 tablespoon chopped parsley
1 tablespoon chopped chives
$\frac{1}{2}$ tablespoon chopped capers

Combine the French dressing with the other ingredients. Mix well. Serve with vegetable, meat and fish salads.

French Dressing with Egg

3 tablespoons olive oil
1 tablespoon vinegar
1 teaspoon mustard
1 hard boiled egg
4 gherkins
Salt and pepper

Combine the olive oil, vinegar and mustard. Mix well. Chop the hard boiled egg and the gherkins. Add to the dressing and season with salt and freshly ground black pepper. Serve with salads.

Anchovy Cream Sauce

250 ml ($\frac{1}{2}$ pint) cream
$1\frac{1}{2}$ teaspoons anchovy paste or Gentlemen's Relish

Mix the anchovy paste with a little of the cream. Whip the remaining cream until stiff. Mix in the anchovy paste. Serve with hot or cold fish.

Basic White Sauce

40 g ($1\frac{1}{2}$ oz.) butter
40 g ($1\frac{1}{2}$ oz.) flour
250–375 ml ($\frac{1}{2}$–$\frac{3}{4}$ pint) milk
Salt and white pepper

This is the basis for many sauces. Melt the butter in a saucepan. Add the flour and mix well. Gradually add the milk, stirring constantly over a medium heat until the sauce is thick and smooth. Bring to the boil and cook for 3 minutes. Season with salt and pepper.

Mustard Sauce

White sauce (see page 217)
2 tablespoons Dijon mustard

Add the mustard to the white sauce. Mix well and serve with boiled, poached or baked fish and eggs.

Sauce Antonia

White sauce (see page 217)
2 tablespoons tomato chutney
1 tablespoon Dijon mustard

Add the tomato chutney and mustard to the white sauce. Mix well and cook for 3 minutes. Serve with baked fish or hard boiled eggs.

Cheese Sauce

50 g (2 oz.) butter
50 g (2 oz.) flour
250–375 ml ($\frac{1}{2}$–$\frac{3}{4}$ pint) milk
1 tablespoon cream
1 egg yolk
50 g (2 oz.) grated cheese
Salt, pepper and paprika

Melt 40 g (1$\frac{1}{2}$ oz.) butter in a saucepan. Add the flour and mix well. Gradually add the milk stirring constantly over a medium heat until the sauce is thick and smooth. Bring to the

boil and remove from the heat. Beat the egg yolk with the
cream. Add to the sauce and heat well. Add 10 g ($\frac{1}{2}$ oz.) butter
and the cheese. Reheat the sauce but do not allow to boil.
Season with salt, pepper and paprika.
 Serve with eggs and fish.

Avocado Sauce

>2 medium avocado pears
>1 teaspoon onion juice, or grated onion
>1 tablespoon lemon juice
>1 tablespoon olive oil
>Salt
>Tabasco sauce

Peel the avocados and remove the stones. Mash the flesh with
the onion juice and lemon juice. Mix until smooth. Gradually
beat in the olive oil, drop by drop. Season with salt and a few
drops of Tabasco sauce. Serve with cold fish and with
shellfish.

Cream and Mustard Dressing

>125 ml ($\frac{1}{4}$ pint) sour cream, or thin cream and lemon juice
>1 tablespoon made English or French mustard
>Salt and pepper

Combine the sour cream with the mustard. Season with salt
and pepper. Serve with vegetables and green salads.

Horseradish Sauce

(1)

>125 ml ($\frac{1}{4}$ pint) double cream
>1 tablespoon freshly grated horseradish
>1 teaspoon lemon juice
>Salt and pepper

Whip the cream until fluffy but not really stiff. Fold in the horseradish and add the lemon juice and seasoning.

(2)

2 tablespoons made horseradish sauce
5 tablespoons double cream
Salt and pepper

Whip the cream until fluffy but not too stiff. Add the horse-radish sauce and season with salt and pepper.

Tomato Sauce

4 tablespoons olive oil
1 peeled and finely chopped onion
1 clove finely chopped or minced garlic
400 g (1 lb.) peeled and chopped tomatoes
1 tablespoon tomato purée
$\frac{1}{2}$ teaspoon sugar
Salt and freshly ground black pepper

Heat the oil in a saucepan. Add the onion and the garlic and cook over a medium heat for 5 minutes. Add the tomatoes, sugar, seasoning, tomato purée, and stir well. Cover and simmer for 10 minutes.

Serve hot with shellfish, fillets of fish, fish fried in batter, etc.

Sour Cream and Mushroom Sauce

250 ml ($\frac{1}{2}$ pint) sour cream
200 g ($\frac{1}{2}$ lb.) button mushrooms
1 tablespoon grated onion
25 g (1 oz.) butter
1 clove garlic
Salt, pepper and paprika

Wash, dry and thinly slice the mushrooms through the stalks and caps. Melt the butter in a saucepan, add the mushrooms and cook for three minutes over a medium heat. Drain and leave to cool. Press the garlic through a garlic press or a fine mincer. Combine the sour cream, mushrooms, onion and garlic. Season with salt, pepper and a pinch of paprika.

Serve with cold mackerel and other cold fish.

Rich Seafood Sauce

250 ml ($\frac{1}{2}$ pint) double cream
2 tablespoons Tomato ketchup
1 teaspoon lemon juice
A few drops of Worcester and Tabasco sauce
Salt and freshly ground black pepper

Whip the cream until firm but not stiff. Mix in the tomato ketchup and lemon juice. Season with a little Worcester sauce, Tabasco sauce, salt and freshly ground black pepper.

Serve chilled with cold fish and cold shellfish.

Note: 2 tablespoons of tomato chutney may be used in place of the tomato ketchup.

Yoghurt Dressing

125 ml ($\frac{1}{4}$ pint) yoghurt
$\frac{1}{2}$ teaspoon lemon juice
1 tablespoon chopped chives
Salt, white pepper and paprika

Combine all the ingredients and mix well. Season with salt, pepper and a pinch of paprika. Serve with cucumber and prawn salads. It also goes well with a lot of meat dishes, Hungarian style.

Whipped Sour Cream and Cucumber Sauce

250 ml ($\frac{1}{2}$ pint) sour cream
$\frac{1}{2}$ cucumber

Salt and freshly ground black pepper
1 teaspoon white wine vinegar
½ teaspoon chopped tarragon or 1 teaspoon tarragon
vinegar

Peel and grate the cucumber. Leave it to drain in a colander
for half an hour. Whip the cream. Add the grated cucumber,
the white wine vinegar and the tarragon. Season with salt and
pepper. Serve with cold fish and shellfish.

CHAPTER FIFTEEN

GARNISHES & ACCOMPANIMENTS

Anchovies
Soak anchovies in milk for half an hour to remove excess saltiness. Use the fillets to decorate egg and fish dishes.

Asparagus
Fresh, boiled or tinned asparagus spears can be used hot to garnish celery dishes in a cream sauce, or cold to garnish mousses, moulds and salads.

Aspic Jelly
Stiff aspic jelly can be chopped into cubes and used to garnish all cold dishes.

Chives
Chopped chives can be used as a decoration and to add taste to cold soups.

Cucumber
Use wafer thin slices of peeled cucumber to decorate all cold dishes.

Dill
Sprays of fresh dill crowns can be used to garnish cold shell-fish dishes. Chopped dill can flavour and decorate cream soups and fish in cream sauces.

Eggs

Hard boiled eggs can be used as a decoration and a garnish in many different forms. Slice hard boiled eggs and make patterns round the edge of cold mousses or fish dishes. Sliced eggs can also be used in the decoration of aspic moulds and jellied dishes. Quartered hard boiled eggs are used as a garnish for salads. Finely chopped hard boiled egg white and yolk gently pressed through a sieve make an attractive decoration for creamed dishes, also a decoration in soups. Used by itself the yolk is known as 'mimosa'.

Gherkins

Can be left whole or cut into fans to decorate cold fish and meat dishes, moulds and mousses. To make gherkin fans make about 6 cuts from the top almost to the bottom of the gherkins, taking care not to cut right through the base, cutting the gherkins into thin slices. Gently spread out into fan shapes.

Lemon

Wafer thin slices of lemon can be used to give taste to and decorate consommés and cream soups. Quarters of lemon should be served with all smoked fish or jellied consommés and fried fish of all varieties.

Mint

Finely chopped mint can be used to decorate and add flavour to cold soups and melon and grapefruit dishes.

Olives

Green and black olives stoned and either left whole, halved or sliced, will decorate fish dishes and salads.

Parsley

Can be used finely chopped, (discard all the stalks), whole in sprigs, or crisply fried in butter. Use fresh chopped parsley for hot egg, fish, vegetable and meat dishes and for soups. Use fresh sprays of parsley for cold fish, egg and meat dishes. Use fried parsley with fried fish.

Peppers (Green and Red)
Cut into thin strips or thin circles, or finely chopped, are a colourful decoration to cold fish dishes and to salads.

Pimentos (Tinned)
Cut into thin strips or finely chopped can be used as a garnish to both hot and cold dishes.

Potatoes
Fluffy creamy mashed potatoes are a good decoration round hot fish dishes in cream sauces. They should preferably be piped through a forcing bag and apart from looking attractive, have the additional asset of making a dish 'stretch'.

Radishes
Whole radishes or radish roses (made like tomato roses – see below) can be used to decorate salads.

Rice
Plain boiled rice or rice mixed with chopped chives and pimento can be used to decorate hot fish dishes.

Tomatoes
Thinly sliced, quartered or cut into roses or lilies can be used to decorate all cold dishes and salads. To make tomato roses use firm tomatoes and a stainless steel knife. Cut each tomato into half and make 4–6 cuts through the tomato almost to the base taking care not to cut right through. Gently fan out the segments. To make tomato lilies make zigzag cuts around the side into the centre of the tomato. Gently pull the two halves apart.

Tomato Aspic
Can be chopped to garnish all cold dishes.

Aspic Jelly

Making one's own aspic jelly is a somewhat complicated process and needs time. I find the commercial aspic crystals very satisfactory, and in emergencies I use tinned consommé. Good stock is essential for any aspic – use fish stock for fish dishes, chicken stock for chicken dishes and meat stock for meat dishes. All aspic is improved by the addition of a tablespoon of sherry or Madeira.

875 ml (1¾ pints) meat or fish stock
125 ml (¼ pint) white wine
50 g (2 oz.) gelatine
2 egg whites

Make sure that the stock is well strained and skim off all grease. Place the stock in a large clean saucepan. Dissolve the gelatine in the wine. Whisk the egg whites until frothy. Add them to the cold stock. Heat slowly whisking with a wire whisk so that the egg whites are well mixed with the stock. Add the wine and gelatine and continue to whisk until the liquid boils. Remove the whisk and boil for ½ minute. Take the saucepan from the stove and leave to settle for 5 minutes. Bring the liquid back to the boil without stirring, then leave to settle again for 5 minutes. Repeat this process once more.

Pour the liquid through a clean muslin cloth. It should be crystal clear. If necessary re-strain it once more. Leave to cool before using.

Note: If the stock is well jellied less gelatine need be used.

Poppy Seed Rolls

8 small bridge rolls
1 beaten egg
1 tablespoon poppy seeds

Brush the rolls with the beaten egg. Sprinkle over the poppy seeds. Place the rolls on a baking sheet. Bake the rolls in a hot oven (230 C., 450 F., Reg. 8) for 5 minutes until crisp and golden brown. Serve hot with butter.

Cheese and Paprika Rolls

8 small bridge rolls
1 beaten egg
2 tablespoons finely grated Cheddar cheese
Salt, pepper, and paprika

Mix the beaten egg with the grated cheese. Season with salt and pepper. Brush the rolls with the cheese mixture and sprinkle a little paprika over the top. Place the rolls on a baking sheet and bake in a hot oven (230 C., 450 F., Reg. 8) for 5 minutes until crisp and golden brown. Serve hot with butter.

Garlic Bread

1 French loaf
100 g (4 oz.) butter
2 cloves crushed garlic

Cut the loaf into thick slices, three quarters of the way through. Soften the butter and mix it with the garlic. Spread the butter on both sides of the bread slices. Press the loaf back into shape. Place on a baking sheet; bake in a hot oven (220 C., 425 F., Reg. 7) until the loaf is crisp and the butter has melted and soaked into the bread, about 8 minutes. Serve with soups.

Cheese Bread

Follow the same method as for garlic bread but use 50 g (2 oz.) grated Parmesan in place of the garlic. Serve very hot with soups and light first courses.

Anchovy Bread

Proceed as for garlic bread but use 1 tablespoon Gentlemen's Relish or mashed anchovies instead of the garlic. Serve very hot; delicious with soups and light first courses.

Garlic Bread with Olive Oil

1 French loaf
3 cloves garlic
1 teaspoon salt
125 ml ($\frac{1}{4}$ pint) olive oil
Black pepper and a little cayenne

Slice the loaf diagonally in 4 cm (1½ inch) slices three quarters of the way through. Press the garlic through a garlic press or mince finely. Combine the garlic with the salt and olive oil. Brush the olive oil between the slices. Pour any remainder over the top. Sprinkle the surface of the loaf with black pepper and a little cayenne. Bake in a hot oven (230 C., 450 F., Reg. 8) for 5–8 minutes until crisp and brown. Serve at once.

Cheese Biscuits

Serve these hot with clear soups.

> 75 g (3 oz.) flour
> 40 g (1½ oz.) butter
> 75 g (3 oz.) grated Cheddar cheese
> Salt, pepper and a pinch of cayenne
> 1 egg yolk

Sift the flour. Add the butter cut into small pieces and rub it into the flour, using your finger tips, until the mixture resembles fine breadcrumbs. Add the cheese and seasoning and mix to a stiff paste with the egg yolk (add a little cold water if the mixture is too dry). Knead the paste for ½ a minute on a lightly floured board. Roll out to 3 mm (⅛ inch) thickness. Cut into rounds with a pastry cutter. Prick the surface with a fork and bake in a moderate oven (180 C., 350 F., Reg. 4) for 10–15 minutes until the biscuits are golden brown.

Heat the biscuits in a moderate oven for 2 minutes before serving.

Cheese and Tomato Toast

Serve with plain soups.

> 4 slices bread
> 25 g (1 oz.) butter
> 2 large tomatoes
> 50 g (2 oz.) grated cheese
> A pinch of cayenne

Remove the crusts from the bread and spread the slices with butter. Cut each slice into 4. Slice the tomatoes. Place a slice of tomato on each square of bread. Cover with grated cheese and sprinkle over a very small amount of cayenne.

Bake the slices in a hot oven (220 C., 425 F., Reg. 7) for 5–8 minutes until the cheese has melted and is lightly browned on the surface.

Cheese Quenelles

100 g ($\frac{1}{4}$ lb.) Cheddar cheese
15 g ($\frac{1}{2}$ oz.) butter
2 eggs
50 g (2 oz.) bread
250 ml ($\frac{1}{2}$ pint) milk
1 tablespoon cream
Salt and pepper

Grate the cheese and mix to a smooth paste with the butter. Beat the eggs and mix with the cheese and butter.

Soak the bread (without crusts) until soft in the milk. Squeeze gently to remove any excess liquid.

Mix the bread with the cream and the cheese mixture. Season with salt and pepper.

Form the mixture into small balls and drop into boiling soup. Boil until the quenelles rise to the surface.

INDEX